VITAL SIGNS

Where Is Your Life Heading?

About the Book

"Keep Away From Children!" "Pay As You Order!" "Drink Moderately!" "No Loitering Allowed!" "Merging Lanes, Give Way!" And many more.

There's more to these commonplace reminders than meets the eye. They bid us all to behave well. Yes, those signboards are meant to awaken in you and me—rational beings—our sense of right and wrong, good and bad.

Moral guideposts are scarce these days while far too many people seem lost in life. So public notices serve to fill in the gaps, reminding us of the ABCs of good manners and right conduct taught in kindergarten.

Classical virtues such as prudence, justice, fortitude, temperance and honesty do not wane. We need them more than ever. If you think modern society has little need of ethics, just look around you!

A simple sign like "Stop, Look & Listen" posted at a railroad crossing, or the label "Drink Moderately" attached to a bottle of cognac, has much to say about our human identity, who we really are, and how we ought to live our lives.

Short and sharp messages. Each contains a wealth of hidden wisdom. These are Vital Signs because they help us face the question every man or woman must answer: "Where is your life heading?" This book is light reading, but be ready for doctrinal punches!

About the Author

FR. HENRY BOCALA is a priest of Opus Dei and a doctor of Canon Law (*Summa cum laude*) from the Pontifical University of the Holy Cross in Rome. He carried out his priestly ministry in Spain, Italy, South Africa, and Israel. He was the Chaplain of Warrane College at the University of New South Wales in Sydney, Australia, before returning to the Philippines in 2003.

Fr. Bocala is the author of *Diplomatic Relations between the Holy See and the State of Israel* (2003), a historical-juridical study; *Arise and Walk* (2007), a compilation of Gospel-based spiritual reflections; and *Mending A Broken Society* (2012), a collection of essays on social-moral issues. *Arise and Walk* in audio-CD format won a special citation from the Catholic Mass Media Awards (Manila, 2011).

Before receiving the Sacrament of Holy Orders, Bocala studied Political Science and worked as a legislative officer in the Philippine Senate. He was also a freelance writer and won multiple awards as an artist. He now works full-time in pastoral ministry among students and young professionals in Manila.

Where Is Your Life Heading?

HENRY BOCALA

Leonine Publishers
Phoenix, Arizona, USA

NIHIL OBSTAT
    Rev. Fr. Ronald M. Roberto
    Asst. Minister for Liturgical Affairs
    Diocese of Cubao, Philippines
    15 April 2015

IMPRIMATUR
    ✠ Most Rev. Honesto F. Ongtioco, D.D.
    Bishop of Cubao, Philippines
    15 April 2015

Copyright © 2015 Henry Bocala

All rights reserved. No part of this book may be reproduced or transmitted in any form or by any means, electronic or mechanical, including photocopying, recording, or by any information storage or retrieval system now existing or to be invented, without written permission from the respective copyright holder(s), except for the inclusion of brief quotations in a review.

All texts of the Sacred Scriptures quoted in this book are taken from *The Catholic Edition of the Revised Standard Version of the Bible*, copyright © 1965, 1966, by the Division of Christian Education of the National Council of the Churches of Christ in the United States of America. Used by permission. All rights reserved.

Cover design by Chris Prufer: pidsdevelopment@gmail.com

        Published by Leonine Publishers LLC
                Phoenix, Arizona
                      USA

ISBN-13: 978-1-942190-15-8
Library of Congress Control Number: 2015947006

10 9 8 7 6 5 4 3 2 1

Visit us online at www.leoninepublishers.com
For more information: info@leoninepublishers.com

CONTENTS

INTRODUCTION 1

CHAPTER ONE
MERGING LANES—GIVE WAY! 7
    Life Lanes 8
    Social Animal 12
    Oasis of Love 15

CHAPTER TWO
KEEP AWAY FROM CHILDREN 21
    Keep Away From Adults 22
    Right Choices 24
    Food for the Soul 27
    Rekindled Embers 30

CHAPTER THREE
STOP, LOOK & LISTEN! 35
    Street-Smart Virtue 36
    Stop, Look & Listen! 39
    Memoria and *Solertia* 43
    Classical Roots 47

CHAPTER FOUR
PAY AS YOU ORDER 51
    Paperclip Integrity 52
    True vs. Bogus Rights 57
    Common Good 61
    Beyond Legal Justice 64

Chapter Five
BREAK GLASS IN CASE OF EMERGENCY 69
    Brave It Out! 70
    Obverse of Weakness. 73
    Fight to Win. 76
    Time to Thole. 79
    Stick to the Good. 81

Chapter Six
DRINK MODERATELY. 85
    From Use to Abuse 86
    Magnet of Pleasure 89
    Healthy Balance. 95
    Wise Label. 101

Chapter Seven
IS IT THE TRUTH? 105
    Calling a Spade, a Spade 107
    Thin Edge of the Wedge 109
    Sine Cera. 112
    Tiny Children 115

Chapter Eight
NO LOITERING ALLOWED 121
    Ut Operaretur. 122
    Do It Now! 124
    Work-Life Balance 128
    Hands, Heart and Head 130

INTRODUCTION

"Keep away from children!"
"Pay-as-you-order!"
"Drink moderately!"
"Break glass in case of emergency!"
"Merging lanes, give way!"
"Stop, Look & Listen!"

We see all kinds of reminders everywhere we go in the form of road signs, product labels, and hazard warnings. They have become so familiar and commonplace we hardly pay them any attention. Yet there is more than meets the eye in these public notices—they help us keep order and stay safe; they bid us all to behave well, short of calling us to a life of virtue.

If we stop to ponder the lessons in those signs, we will realize that they appeal to our rationality and moral sense. Why? Because that's what we are—self-knowing and intelligent beings who think and make choices—based on our sense of right and wrong. If we take to heart those signs, we're on the right track. No, they don't elaborate on what we need to do in order to shape up. They are no-frills, straightforward ads that try to guide people's conduct a bit. Besides, "God willed that man should be left in the hand of his own counsel." (Sir 15:14)

When moral resources are scarce, simple signs like "Wait for your turn!" or "CCTV in operation!" are a great help, if not a must. The first implies that we should follow order while the second warns us not to mess around. Somehow we need to be re-educated on the ABCs of good manners and right conduct taught in kindergarten. Those signs have much to say about our human identity: who we really are and how we ought to live our life.

These direct, simple, laconic messages contain a whole lot of hidden wisdom. They are short because they are intended for a reader in a swift-moving vehicle or a person in a hurry. They are concise in order to get the message across in an instant, and succinct because the rest is common sense, we're supposed to be mature, capable of sound judgments.

Have you ever been to an accident site or crime spot? The police often cordons off the area with pastel-colored duct tape or a plastic band on which is printed: "Crime Scene, Do Not Cross!" Which means: "Keep off!" or "Stay away!" Some years ago a powerful explosion shook a resort and night club district, killing over two hundred people, mostly tourists. But it was preceded by a minor blast. Whoever planted the bombs seemed to capitalize on human *fear* and *curiosity*. Because the initial blowup was meant to draw the crowd to the area, and when pandemonium ensued even as prying eyes huddled in the vicinity, the really big bang came. The ploy maximized casualties. There might not have been time for police to secure the area before the second detonation. But the point is, where it appears, police duct tape carries a little moral lesson.

So is the case with notifications like "Fragile, handle with care!" "No Loitering Allowed!" "Slow down, children crossing!" "No ID, No Entry!" "Don't leave your valuables unattended!" "Yellow hat zone!" "Flammable. No smoking within 50 feet!" You can add many others. Each message talks to you and me as responsible individuals.

Though the indices are there mainly for regulatory purposes rather than to convince us to be good, they certainly foster virtues and hence, help us all become better persons. Social order is built on values and ultimately on human virtues. "Pay as you order" actually reminds us of our duty of justice. By extension it also means, "Settle your debt!" Or "Return what you borrow!" Or "Be considerate to others!" "Drink moderately!" exhorts us to be sober, temperate and exercise self-control in anything we find pleasurable. "Stop, Look & Listen!" is another way of saying, "Be prudent and careful, seek advice, learn from the past, think things over, and don't be reckless!" And so on and so forth.

It's not society's role, of course, to produce saints. You never see placards that say, "Be honest!" or "Be chaste!" in the malls, parks and subways. By nature, the state or public authorities are minimalist ethics wise. The task of character formation properly belongs to the family, school and the church. Public officials do no more than ensure general order.

In medical parlance the phrase *vital signs* refers to measures of basic physiological functions like heartbeat, body temperature, blood pressure and breathing rate. In other words, the state of physical health. In this book, however, I take the liberty to use the term *Vital Signs* figuratively to mean *guides* to spiritual health that appear as product *labels*, street *signs*, policy *notices* and the like. What's the connection? Well, the human person is a composite of flesh and spirit, body and soul, the latter being the principle of life.

What inspired me to write *Vital Signs* are the lack of clear direction in many people's lives and the dearth of moral guideposts in our confused times. Society's good old values are gone. Role models are few and far between. Many ethical systems have no legs to stand on. The fine line between good and bad is blurred, let alone rubbed out. If you want to look for a moral compass amidst a desert of relativism, here's wishing you good luck! It would be like looking for rare earth minerals.

Truly valuable materials like books of virtues (were they to be found) are gathering dust in the shelves. Few bother to read them and fewer still share what they read. Meanwhile the man in the street is groping in the dark. So the slightest cue or aid to human conduct to be had must be treasured. The most rudimentary roadmap to personal growth is worth looking into. These are the *Vital Signs* we often take for granted. I invite you to discover the nuggets of wisdom they contain. Every chapter of the book discusses a virtue, taking off from a corresponding signage that may not mean much *extempore*, but when understood from another perspective, offers a good deal of human values. This book is light reading, but get ready for doctrinal punches!

We explore the outside world a lot. Yet we know too little of ourselves. Round the clock we're bustling with activities, hopping from one thing to another. We surf the Internet, hang out with friends, buy stuff, read newspapers, drive around, trim the garden or play sports. We seem to be full of life, but only on the surface. Beneath that activism is a gaping hole of inner emptiness. That's why so many people try to appear happy and fulfilled, but deep within they are troubled.

Introduction

The fast pace of modern life leaves little room for reflection. Countless images clutter our mind. There's a frenzy to get to the top and seek material comfort. If only we could take time out to pause and examine ourselves, we would discover our interior life, thoughts, emotions, beliefs and values—in short, the heart's yearnings for a truly meaningful life.

Offhand, the *Vital Signs* we see in every corner are plain official rules that guide everybody's outward manners. But they also point to our interior self, giving directions to the faculties and tendencies of our soul. So next time you drive along the motorway, eat in a restaurant, shop for groceries or open a bottle of Cognac, watch out for those *Vital Signs!* They're principles to live by, pointers for self-fulfillment. They help you face the question every man or woman must answer: "Where is your life heading?"

Rev. Fr. Henry P. Bocala
Manila, 1 November 2014
Solemnity of All the Saints

Chapter One

MERGING LANES— GIVE WAY!

Traffic rules and driving codes are well established in most places, but the real situation out there on the roads can be a lot more complex than the most elaborate guidelines. You might have experienced driving at full speed along a freeway when suddenly you catch sight of a road sign ahead that says: MERGING LANES, GIVE WAY! Your peripheral vision tells you that a car is moving equally fast along a semi-parallel track on your right that joins your lane farther down the road.

Who has the right of way? Would you slow down and let the other motorist pull in front of you? Some say the car on the right always has priority. Others suggest that users of the tributary road must wait. Still others think that whoever is ahead should go first. Well, perhaps the answer is a smart blend of all these.

Adjust your velocity, step on the brakes or speed up if needed! Here reflex and intuition are very crucial because regardless of the traffic regulation, the general rule stands that one should avoid collision even if he or she is in the right place at the right moment. Caution and common sense can spare us from fatal mishaps.

Over and above the norms of traffic safety, there are rules of courtesy or dictates of charity that civilized people ought to follow. They're not written nor codified. They're engraved in the human heart. Behind the steering wheel of every moving vehicle is a warm body, a person who, regardless of his temperament, social etiquette and driving skills, deserves a little understanding, a modicum of charity.

Life Lanes

Metaphorically, our journey through life is full of "merging lanes." Every day we cross paths with all sorts of people at home, in the office, in school, in the public squares, in the hallways and byways of the modern world. We constantly meet and interact with various individuals for reason of work, family, business, education, religion, health and recreation. We find ourselves in different "crossways" round the clock. Our personal lane brings us face to face with countless men and women.

We must be careful then, so as not to step on another's toes, block someone's way, box him out or force him to an abrupt halt. And if we are the ones wronged, let it pass if you can. It's not worth making a big fuss over a tiff and blow things out of proportion. That would be below your dignity, besides spoiling your day. In highway parlance, that's like exploding into road rage just because the vehicle beside you nearly hit your bumper at a curve. Be extra patient! You'll get over it soon. Focus on important matters!

People who live together or work together cannot entirely avoid little conflicts. Frictions are bound to happen simply because we think differently or we hold diverse opinions or my way of doing things is not exactly your style—and there are folks who can't seem to accept that. Disagreements are quite normal in human relations. We are not stacks of dollar bills liked by everybody all the time, even if we try to please everyone. We live in an imperfect world.

We can be very careful when we drive and still run the risk of disaster because the roads out there are strewn with reckless wheelmen. An American study using a car simulator exam showed that "some men develop a passion for driving that can verge on the obsessive. They consider cars to be an extension of themselves and they become aggressive if they are honked at or cut off."[1] Obtrusive driving is some people's way of projecting their hyper-masculinity, propped up by a culture steeped in macho stereotypes. These motorists form one category of "road liabilities."

Do we fall into this bracket? Are we on the watch list of highway patrols? If so, the problem lies in our character traits. On or off road we can easily run into trouble if we don't rein in our arrogant manners, sarcastic comments, air of self-righteousness and penchant to make life difficult for others.

The roads would be a little bit safer then if you just stay home. But go, drive anyway! Drive if you need to, through the crossroads of your habitual occupations because it is through our frequent dealings with others that we can grow in the virtue of charity. Only be more considerate from now on. That caustic remark is better left unsaid, or we might regret its ugly consequences. A snobbish air or cold treatment can put us on a collision course (even sans the noise of words), so better be polite and courteous. We might have the knack for interrupting people when they talk. If you want to butt in, do so gracefully! Perhaps we aren't used to being contradicted. It gets on our nerves. Well, it's healthy to be open-minded and democratic. We wouldn't like to be branded as a hothead yelling and screaming in public. Stay cool! Our boiling blood must simmer down before we react. It pays to say "I'm sorry" especially when we're truly wrong. Then let's strive to polish our abrasive character!

Beware of the devil's maxim that says: "Think ill of someone and you'll fall short." A friend of mine was jolted when an SUV skidded onto his lane, forcing him to swerve and momentarily lose control. Furious, he quickly stopped, flung the door of his BMW wide open and dashed to confront the "bastard" whose car had screeched to a stop. "Drunk driver again, damn it!" he roared. Instead, he got the shock of his life when he found out that the guy had suffered a severe heart attack. He rushed the fellow to a nearby hospital, pricked by remorse of conscience: "Rascal! So quick to judge others." The stranger died in his arms.

MERGING LANES, GIVE WAY. Seen in a positive light, "merging lanes" are not a threat to us. Nor do they signal a potential rivalry, or an occasion of discord, or a cause of disunity. To merge lanes is to share common interests with others, enjoy their company, welcome their inputs, offer whatever we have, work together and support each other. In the merging lanes of daily life, we learn to build rather than destroy, bridge rather than separate.

In some motorways one finds a variance of "Give Way!" The road sign says, "Yield!" That's what we do when we excuse others of their faults, listen to people needing attention, let others take the best share and cheer up friends who are dejected. So too, we "yield" when we forgive, take on a difficult job, lend a helping hand, offer consolation, and rise above petty squabbles. Sometimes we must "merge lanes" if we're in a position to restore harmony where there is strife, to drown hatred in the wellspring of love.[2] As we can see, "Merging Lanes, Give Way" can mean a thousand and one manifestations of charity in our day-to-day life.

It's okay to get a little bit delayed even if it tests the limit of our patience. Better to arrive slightly late but safe and sound, than rush at the risk of ending up in the ICU, if not in a crematorium. So also it's okay to "give way" in the "merging lanes" of human exchange, even if it hurts our pride. Better to "lose" a slight advantage and preserve our warm relations, than be ahead at the cost of estranged friendships. Defensive driving has untold merits. Human discretion has incalculable value.

How we wish perhaps that our lane would never merge or intersect with someone else's, that we could have the long, wide road all to ourselves. Certainly we could do our routine tasks faster without interruption if nobody ever bothers us. We would be spared of annoyances caused by a nagging wife, tyrannical boss, know-it-all colleague, impertinent neighbor or arrogant client—if we shut ourselves in our room 24/7. But that would not be real life.

Highways are for everyone licensed to drive, men and women, rich and poor, young and old, white and black, healthy and sick, smart and dumb. Charity doesn't discriminate, it's a pathway made for everybody. Better still, it opens the way for others. Our duties of charity stem from the fact that we are all members of the human family, radically equal, endowed with common dignity, made in the *image and likeness of God*

(Cf. Gen 1:26-27) and redeemed by the blood of Christ. That is the incalculable worth of our neighbor even if we don't know his or her name.

When we know how to love, we learn to appreciate different character traits. Friendships and human relations in general thrive on variety. "We need the lively, bubbling person who enlivens any gathering. We need the warm-hearted, outgoing person who gives a lift to our spirit. We need the active, go-go person who moves us to get things done. We need the quiet, introspective person whose companionship is so restful and relaxing. We need the sober, deliberate person to whom we may turn for counsel in time of perplexity."[3] There's a place for everybody in this world.

Social Animal

The human person is a social being by nature. Like the song says, "no man is an island; no man stands alone." We are not self-sufficient beings; we need others. "To go out of ourselves and join others is healthy for us. To be self-enclosed is to taste the bitter poison of immanence, and humanity will be worse for every selfish choice we make."[4]

In *Nicomachean Ethics* the Greek philosopher Aristotle said that a man may have everything in this world but he will never be truly happy if he has no friends. As rational creatures, we possess the innate quality to communicate and live with other individuals. In fact, we develop as a person only in so far as we interact with our friends, kinsfolk, peers, and people in general. We don't mature in a social vacuum. Solidarity is a natural vocation of the human person. One's personality is enriched through human relations. It's no surprise that among the most cruel forms of torment is to confine a man in a tiny cubicle. He may have water and food, but cut off from human community, he'll go crazy.

Try living alone on an island and before long you'll lose your mind. This is a silly proposition, I admit. But isn't it true that in the urban jungle so many people choose to live in isolation? That's the paradox of modern life. Take the case of social networking. Facebook, for example, has the amazing capacity to reconnect us with long-lost friends. The world has truly become a global village, thanks to the facility of advanced info-technology. Ironically, we can become so absorbed with on-line chats, on-line games or web surfing as to ignore the fellow next to us. There's nothing like face-to-face interactions and live chats. And so much the better if it's over a cup of coffee.

Hi-tech tools of communication do not automatically bring us closer to each other. Even the fastest wi-fi connections won't take a digital native out of his eggshell and comfort zone if he chooses to remain within his enclave. Charity and solidarity do not come from silicon chips and microprocessors. Virtues reside in the human heart and in the human mind. Self-centeredness and indifference can only be overcome by a firm disposition to be with others and to do something worthwhile for them. Contemporary society is markedly individualistic and narcissistic. No wonder in the hubbub of a great metropolis there are so many lonely and depressed people, whereas a village farmer can be so content, happy and close to his nearest neighbor who resides a mile away.

We can't love our fellowmen just by mingling with them. Nor is charity reduced to spurts of compassion shown in almsgiving to the poor. Charity is a stable habit of seeking the good of others. It's proactive, constantly finding ways to serve. The virtue may occasionally call for heroic acts such as pulling a victim of an accident out of a wrecked, ill-fated car. It may also require policy directions that lighten the burdens of developing nations and improve the plight of billions of people mired in poverty. But these are rare. It's in the "motorway" of daily life where our kindness is really seen in the form of a small act of service, a warm greeting, an act of gratitude, a well-meaning correction, a word of comfort, an assurance of support or a silent prayer for someone.

Seeking the good of others: that's fraternal charity in a nutshell. When we help someone or treat him kindly because we expect something in return or stand to gain by so doing, we're being selfish, not selfless. There's no love in service done for sordid motives, carried out with a mercenary mindset. Gifts with strings attached are a bane, not a boon. True love is altruistic, the kind that people have who share the little that they have, forgive those who hurt them, or give anonymous donations. Generosity touches people's hearts and stirs up their good dispositions.[5]

A gentle, elderly Spanish widow living alone in an apartment posted a hand-written note by the elevator. "Lost, 500-peseta bill. If found, please return to Mrs. Castrillo, Apartment 6A." She received but a meager pension from the government, so she needed badly the amount she lost. One fellow took pity on her, knocked on her door (she was already hard of hearing so it took her time to come and open) and when she came out, handed her the money. "Oh, what luck! Thank you very much, my son," the old lady beamed with misty eyes. He played along, pretending that he had found the money. Two days later, he needed to have some clothes ironed so he phoned her (she offered this service to augment her little income). She excitedly told him that three other residents of the building, all claiming to have found her 500-peseta bill, came at different times to give her the cash. When she declined, they all insisted she take it. "And you know what," she laughed, "I found the missing bill in my bath robe. Could you please be kind enough to remove the sign by the elevator? Somebody else might find my money again."[6]

Oasis of Love

A kind-hearted person is like an oasis of love in a desert of social apathy, a touch of gentleness in a rude world. Only a few, if any, would notice his or her acts of benevolence because they're discreet. Goodness is like his second nature. By force of habit, almost effortlessly, he opens the door for others. He doesn't mind sitting at the back. He helps an old man cross the street. He serves others at meals. He says "thank you" to the cab driver. He spends time to tutor his little kid. He sends a birthday greeting to a colleague. He gives generous tips to the handyman. He begs for unnecessary apologies. He shows keen interest in a troubled friend. He smiles at everyone he meets. And a myriad other gestures of kindness! Charity is the synthesis of all good works.[7]

One naturally feels attracted to persons of goodwill because of their refined manner, good humor, friendly smile, encouraging remark, kind consideration, fair judgment, readiness to help, positive thinking and rare candor. United to the truth, charity is an authentic expression of humanity and an indispensable element in human relations.[8]

Charitable individuals have a big heart, big enough to make room for the likable and the "unlikable" alike. They always have nice words to say about others. Men of heart can lavish care and attention upon those disdained by others. When offended, they are quick to forgive and forget. We feel comfortable in their presence. They're the ones who listen when everybody else chooses to lend a deaf ear. They're the ones who welcome when everyone else closes the door. They're the ones who lift you up when all the others let you down.

That's what the Good Samaritan did in the parable Jesus told us in the Gospel. Recall the story: a traveller from Jerusalem to Jericho was robbed, beaten up and left unconscious along the road. A priest came by and avoided the victim. Then a Levite passed by, but he too, ignored the half-dead man. Finally, a Samaritan appeared. It was this stranger who showed compassion for the injured. He took care of him, bandaged his wounds, carried him, brought him to an inn and made sure the poor fellow would be taken good care of. (Cf. Lk 10:29-37)

I have been in both cities. They are just 23 miles apart, but their difference in terms of elevation is notable. Jerusalem is 650 to 840 meters above sea level, while Jericho is 260 meters below sea level, making it the lowest city on the planet. The road that links the two places is downhill and winding. Figuratively, we can say that the man described in the parable was journeying from a high point to a low point, descending towards misfortune. He would have bled to death probably if not for the Good Samaritan. The first ones who merged lanes with the hapless traveller attacked him. The next two turned a blind eye. The fourth succored him. Merging lanes, as we can see, can be an occasion to hurt someone, or treat him coldly and with indifference, or come to his aid. Jesus narrated the parable precisely to teach us all a lesson on fraternal charity.

> Love is patient and kind; love is not jealous or boastful; it is not arrogant or rude. Love does not insist on its own way; it is not irritable or resentful; it does not rejoice at wrong, but rejoices in the right. Love bears all things, believes all things, hopes all things, endures all things. (1 Cor 13:4-7)

A person who truly loves—with an authentic and untarnished love—would seek every opportunity to "merge lanes" with others, not so as to meddle in their affairs, but to help in whatever way possible. No burden is too much if it's a question of lifting up someone who has fallen due to poverty, sickness, abandonment, moral dilemma or spiritual crisis. The person consumed by Christian love doesn't balk at obstacles to do something good for others. He or she has a broad perspective, a universal outlook, and a vision that transcends narrow horizons. A charitable fellow has an uncanny capacity to detect the needs of others and come to their aid. We may not be the smartest or the most talented guy or gal in town, but when we know how to love, we possess the single most important thing in life. Saint Augustine masterfully put it when he said: "Love and do what you will; if you are quiet, be quiet for love; if you speak, speak for love; if you correct, correct for love; if you forgive, forgive for love…"[9]

When you are kind, you put others in your place because we naturally love and treat ourselves well. Kindness adds sweetness to everything. "The secret impulse out of which kindness acts is an instinct that is the noblest part of yourself. It is the most undoubted remnant of the image of God, given to us at the beginning." It "springs from the soul of man."[10] To be kind, to do acts of charity, is to imitate no less than Our Lord Jesus Christ who commands us to "love the Lord your God with all your heart, and with all your soul, and with all your strength, and with all your mind" and to love "your neighbor as yourself." (Lk 10:27)

So next time you see the road sign MERGING LANES, take it as an invitation for you to love and to live charity, and life will smile on you. For *Ubi caritas et amor, Deus ibi est*—"Where there is charity and love, there is God."[11]

---

[1] http://www.sciencedaily.com/releases/2010/05/100526111332.htm.

[2] St. Josemaría Escrivá, *The Forge*, no. 564.

[3] Leo J. Trese, *Human But Holy: Getting To Know God, Yourself and Your Neighbor*. Manila: Sinag-Tala Publishers, Inc., 1999, p. 93.

[4] Pope Francis, *Evangelii Gaudium* (2013), no. 87.

[5] Linda Kavelin Popov, *The Family Virtues Guide*. New York: Penguin Group, 1997, p. 134.

[6] Ignatius Segarra, *The Race of the Century*. Manila: Sinag-Tala Publishers, Inc., 1994, p. 58.

[7] *Catechism of the Catholic Church*, no. 1829.

[8] Benedict XVI, *Caritas In Veritate* (2009), no. 3.

[9] Commentary on the First Epistle of St. John, 7, 9. Text in Juan Luis Lorda, *The Virtues of Holiness: The Basics of Spiritual Struggle*. New York: Scepter Publishers, Inc., 2010, p. 64.

[10] Lawrence Lovasik, *The Hidden Power of Kindness: A Practical Handbook for Souls Who Dare to Transform the World, One Deed at a Time*. Manchester: Sophia Institute Press, 1999, pp. 5-6.

[11] From the antiphon sung during the ceremony of the Washing of the Feet at the Mass of the Last Supper on Holy Thursday.

Chapter Two

KEEP AWAY FROM CHILDREN

Keep away from children! You see this cautionary label in a lot of consumer goods and household products, from kerosene to paper glue to duct tape to insecticide to nail polish—for obvious reason. Kids are ignorant of the potential hazards posed by these items. Being playful and innocent, little boys and girls can choke on baking flour, cut their fingers with the kitchen knife, drink shampoo or burn the house with matchsticks. If children mess around, it's really our fault. They don't know what they're doing, do they? We know better and we're expected to be on top of things. So products contain warning labels lest toddlers get into trouble due to sheer negligence on our part.

Here is an example. A mother stepped out of the house for a moment to open the gate, and when she got back three minutes later her little John, a 5-year-old hyperactive ADHD boy, was already toasting a pair of bathroom slippers in the microwave oven. Just a few days earlier the same child made a toy boat out of a piece of paper he took from atop a desk that turned out to be a Deed-of-Sale; the notarized sheet went floating around the pool. Both the slippers and the document are in fact harmless, but we can be surprised at what kids—creatures with no full use of reason—can do with this stuff. Little John's "mischiefs" may or may not bode ill for the kind of man he'll become in the future. For now though, his guardians would have to bear the brunt of the consequences of the mishaps he causes.

Keep Away From Adults

How about a label that says: Keep away from adults. Have you ever seen one? Of course there is none. You may ask, "Where's that supposed to be attached anyway?" Unless they're drunk, drugged, or deranged, adults know too well where, when and how to use flour, kerosene, paper glue, duct tape, insecticide and nail polish. Yet there's a different kind of danger for grown up men and women that hardly affects the children, precisely because the former "know" what they're doing, while the latter are totally clueless—until they too, come of age.

I refer to moral pollutants that fill every nook and cranny of our society. They're all over, part of modern life, embedded in customs and institutions, acceptable to large segments of the populace and even extolled as signs of progress and "hallmarks" of a free society. Nobody is immune from these spiritual contaminants. Even people of unquestioned probity are exposed to them much like passive smokers who unwillingly inhale nicotine puffed out by cigarette users.

We hardly find any signs to caution us against moral hazards. Yet these poison the human spirit and spoil the core of our being. This may sound absurd, but I like to imagine a time when such a warning sign—"Keep away from adults"—in bold, conspicuous letters, are pasted on illegal drugs, porn, abortion pills, blasphemous materials and the like. Perhaps a similar signage but bigger—like those attached to high-voltage wires and fences—should be hanged at the entrance of girly bars and strip clubs, sensual spa and massage parlors, but also in bare-knuckle brawl cages and child trafficking dens, if we can find them.

Silly? Nonsensical? Old-fashioned? Not so if we're really honest with ourselves. Have you ever wondered why tobacco, alcohol, gambling and, in some places, even coffee and soft drinks are labeled as "sin" products and why a sumptuary tax is levied on them? It's pretty simple. These are socially undesirable products and services; they are proscribed by society due to their unhealthy nature; and they are curbed by state laws to "compel" people to change their behavior—somehow. Just imagine the inimical effects of products and services that are downright immoral!

Like so many people, perhaps we just shrug off the idea in a gesture of apathy. But deep down we know too well that certain things peddled in the market inflict real, serious harm on individuals and families. They may appear cool, fun and chic, but they wreck havoc on us much as termites can burrow deep into wooden panels. Bit by bit they make us greedy, lustful, gluttonous, slothful, envious, materialistic, vengeful, irreverent and dishonest. "You slake your senses and faculties in whatever pool you meet on the way. And you can feel the results: unsettled purpose, scattered attention, deadened will and quickened concupiscence."[1]

What an irony it would be if a child were to rebuke an adult instead of the other way around! That's exactly what happened to a family I know of. Their youngest child, a 9-year-old boy, told his dad as he slouched on the sofa to watch a slatternly, late-night TV show: "You're not supposed to watch that, Daddy," he said as he positioned himself right in front of the TV to cover it with his outstretched arms. The father was taken aback and prodded his son to go to bed, but thought better of it and pricked by a remorse of conscience, changed the channel.

The TV, Internet, smartphones and DVDs are not bad of course. They're awesome work tools and a veritable source of entertainment. But they can also be destructive. It all depends on the user, on the disposition of one's heart. We can click on web links, for example, that either give wisdom or trash, prayer or pornography, tranquility or violence. No amount of filter will protect us better than the buffer of self-control.

Cheap pleasures beguile us into thinking these can make us truly happy. Right reason is often trumped by the thrill of instant gratification, thanks to the complicity of our base instincts and secular environment. We often jump at something we would soon regret, swayed by a fleeting emotion, and lacking a set of criteria possessed by mature individuals. We need to make the right choices in life. If it were simply choosing an ice cream flavor or a shoe brand it would not matter much. But think twice or thrice when you're about to do something that could make you either a better or a worse person.

Right Choices

How our life unfolds, our joys and sorrows, blessings and miseries, are for the most part consequences of the choices we make. True, circumstances may condition our freedom to some degree; there are situations we can't totally avoid. Still, we are basically what we make of ourselves especially in the moral sphere. "In all decisions there is a point at which we freely choose to tip the scales in one direction or another... For the normal person there is that margin of freedom, however narrow, wherein we have to speak our own 'yes' or 'no.'"[2] We shape our own future, we write our own biography, and we choose our own destiny. "I have set before you life and death, blessing and curse; therefore choose life that you...may live." (Deut 30:19)

Talking about right choices, it's not easy to find a moral compass nowadays. Many people are at a loss, lacking clear direction in life. Value formation is scarce and there's widespread ignorance about healthy moral living. Young persons are generally left to fend for themselves, spiritually that is. Of course there are still families that function as schools of virtues. But they are fewer each time. For the rest, *cada caminante siga su camino* (each wayfarer follows his own path), as the Spanish dictum says. We thus need to carry in our hearts a set of standards that serves as a prism through which we discern what's valuable and what's trash. It takes a principled individual to detect the threats to our moral life, threats that assail us in ways both subtle and blunt, in small doses of poison or in a torrent of filth.

Good character is what provides a firm anchor amidst the ebb and flow of consumerist tides, a stable point of reference in the maelstrom of modern paganism. Moral indicators should be found within "me." It's up to us to hang it on the walls of a delicate, well-formed conscience. Bankrupt culture in fact reminds us of the need to build an armor of values and spiritual reserve to shield us against the juggernaut of secularism. It's so easy to follow the crowd, to go with the flow and just do what everyone else is doing. Conformism is a convenient way to let others lead the way and do the thinking for us. But when we blindly follow in their footsteps even all the way to the moral precipice, that's sheer madness. We've got to have the spine and the guts to go against the grain and stand up for our beliefs.[3]

The labels that forewarn us of impending danger should be in our eyes, heart, reason and will. They should pop out by force of habit, fruit of one's maturity, sound judgment, upright conscience, moral discernment and interior life. No. We won't allow the market to determine our choices. Life—the only one we have in this world—is too precious to just leave in the hands of dark, unscrupulous forces.

We find wise tips or friendly reminders like "cigarette smoking is dangerous to your health" or "if symptoms persist, consult your doctor." These stickers help ensure our physical safety, period. So do warning signs like "slippery when wet," "flammable, no smoking within 50 feet" and "beware of attack dogs."

How come we have all sorts of warnings against bodily harm, yet we wear no protection against moral threats? It's actually a rhetorical question. The answer is pretty simple. Not so many people really care about the spiritual-moral life. We are too engrossed in worldly concerns—staying physically fit, looking pretty or handsome, amassing wealth, building up our credentials, booking in resort-hotels, hanging out with friends, trimming our gardens, washing our cars, grooming our pets. Occasionally perhaps we mumble a few bedtime prayers and drop by the church, but these religious gestures are no more than lip service, little more than a semblance of spirituality to appease the Divinity.

Healthy living is not all about diets, exercise, vitamins, rest and medicine. We surely do well if we monitor our calorie intake, take food supplements, get enough sleep and do regular workouts. These are necessary, but not enough. Nor are they the most important things in life. They would be—if we were just a motley collection of nerves, muscles and bones; if the highest goal we could ever have were earthly success, let alone physical fitness. But the human person is a lot more than a two-legged animal. You and I are bio-physical, psycho-social and moral-spiritual beings. All-in-one, a multi-faceted unity. That's what we all are.

The human person is a kind of a bridge. He is the vital link between "the material world and the spiritual world...and (he) thus occupies a special place in the matrix of the created order."[4] We have the unique responsibility, so to speak, to unite creation, incarnating spirit in ourselves and, conversely, lifting material being up to God—thereby, all in all, contributing to the great symphony of creation.[5]

Food for the Soul

Try visiting your favorite bookshop. All over the shelves you see an array of self-help, personality-enriching and success-unlocking formula books. They talk about the power of positive thinking, sure steps to excellence and the secrets to success. Most of these self-improvement books are "best-sellers" and in many ways bear witness to the spiritual side of the human person. They simply couch in layman's terms our spiritual and moral needs. "Slug it out" is a popular way of saying, "persevere in your good resolutions." "Self-acceptance heals" might just be another way of telling us that "it's important to be humble." "How to win friends" actually gives you tips on how to live charity better. "Treasure moments of silence in reflective solitude" is a polite approach to convince us that we should set aside time for prayer.

We don't even have to look for external proofs of the reality of our spiritual dimension. It's enough to examine our own life. Our past timeline probably shows an array of frustrations, doubts, anger, disappointments, sadness, anxieties, bitterness, resentments, disgust, pride and hatred. But just as true, we also have a fair share of joys, compassion, healing, peace, understanding, mercy, humility and love—profound experiences that point to the spiritual facet of every human being.

What about our desire for freedom, independence, respect for honor and dignity? And our innate tendency to seek truth, beauty, goodness, fulfillment, meaning and love? Aren't all these innate yearnings of the inner self? Voices of the human soul? The spiritual soul is everybody's better half, men and women alike, the nobler part of human life. The primacy of the spiritual over the physical is not a propaganda. It's affirmed in the sacred scriptures. For "what will it profit a man, if he gains the whole world and forfeits his life?" (Mt 16:26)

That other hemisphere, the spiritual half of the human person, similarly needs nourishment. Just as there's food for the body, so also there's food for the soul. If you're still in the bookshop, look closely at the section on Inspirational and Motivational books. There you'll probably find a nicely bound manual on Yoga, Scientology or Transcendental Meditation with a free DVD that shows you the technique on how to practice them. They sell like the proverbial hot cakes, patronized by overstressed folks who are looking for ways to gather their scattered senses, recollect their dissipated minds and quiet their restless souls. Behind such longing for peace is the quest for the Absolute. It's the secular world's unconscious attempt to search for light and life's meaning amidst darkness and confusion.

The modern man is unknowingly searching for God. History has come full circle, for this trend is not something new. Over two thousand years ago many pagans had the same dilemma. They were groping in the dark until St. Paul, the Apostle of the Gentiles, brought them *Lumen Christi* (Light of Christ). Standing in the midst of the Aeropagus, Paul of Tarsus addressed the Athenians in the following words: "Men of Athens, I perceive that in every way you are very religious. For as I passed along, and observed the objects of your worship, I found also an altar with this inscription, 'To an unknown god.' What therefore you worship as unknown, this I proclaim to you." (Acts 17:22-23)

You're still in front of the shelf that showcases pseudo-psycho-religious concoctions. Many of these are not real food for the soul, but only reminders that you've got a soul. So walk farther down the aisle. Skip those items that you don't probably need like watercolors, fountain pens, computer software and gadgets that can be found in those colossal bookstores.

But when you come to the section on General Spirituality or Moral Treatises, you've got to stop and pay attention. Here customer differentiation seldom applies, if at all. Because we all have something to learn from the wisdom and rich experience spiritual books contain, those that truly help us shape up. While not all of us are painters or computer wizards or executives, all of us form attitudes, practice certain habits, develop character traits and adopt lifestyles that often need sculpting and tidying up, if not a total overhaul. Not everyone cares about art and IT programs, but all of us—absolutely all individuals—stand to benefit from whatever helps us grow as a person, body and soul.

If you're not sure which materials are good for you, ask a spiritual director with rich experience in guiding souls, or click on reliable websites to check the catalog of worthy readings. You may not exactly like Encyclicals or Catechisms, but don't be too quick to brush them aside. This type of books contains sure doctrine. You just have to think a little deeper to appreciate the rich wisdom they offer. By all means, you can start with easy-to-read, inspiring, popular paperbacks as long as they form, not deform you. (The latter include books that feed human vanity and put high premium on wealth, beauty and fame as the primary gauge of success. Their message is that money and power are what save us, not God).

Rekindled Embers

Our spiritual needs vary. Yet in one way or another, we all need conversion, forgiveness, change and maturity. We might have suffered painful wounds in the past that take time to heal. Perhaps we haven't gotten over some little tragedies in life. There were times maybe when we felt that the burden was too much to bear. But then we hang on to the fragile remnants of faith in us;

we renewed the dwindling hope imbedded deep in our hearts, we reawakened our latent capacity to love. We didn't want to admit it; we didn't want people to notice it, but we knew deep within that God was calling us to return home. We used to hate praying. We abhorred the idea that we're sinners. But now, after wandering aimlessly in the desert of worldliness and disbelief, we have discovered an oasis of love in God, the source of living water, the only place where life can be sustained. It has dawned on us that our earthly journey is worthwhile only if we walk with a perspective of eternity. We have long deprived our soul of inner peace, the peace that only Christ can give, until the disillusions of life rekindled in us the embers of God's love.

At long last, we have finally found the courage to straighten the twists and bends, warps and creases in our life. We're now ready to purify our heart, approach the doctor of souls, undo the errors of our youth, leave behind the old self, reshape our lives, change our attitude, adjust our lifestyle, root out bad habits, cultivate human and Christian virtues, make a fresh start, redirect our plans, seek God's pardon and grace: in a word, become a new person, conscious of one's dignity as a child of God.

Conversion, though, is not the end of a process. It's the beginning, the start of a new life. That life is meant to grow through the practice of virtues, the habit of prayer and active sacramental life—three strands of thread which, interwoven with our daily work form, as it were, the tightly-knit fabric of a mature human and Christian life. We are mature when we do what we're supposed to do and shun what we must avoid, when we no longer act like immature children who are "tossed to and fro and carried about with every wind of doctrine, by the cunning of men, by their craftiness in deceitful wiles." (Eph 4:14)

I hate saying the obvious, but let's say it anyway. Kids go to the toy section because they like toys. Mom and dad go there, I suppose, to buy toys for their kids and not because they want to fly RC (remote-controlled) choppers or piece together Lego models. Now if four or five year-old boys and girls are in front of FHM or Maxim magazines, they're probably lost in the labyrinth of a department store. But not so when you see 20- or 30- or 40-something year olds loitering there. Chances are, base instincts led them there—to satisfy their curiosity, indulge in their passions. The kids found in these zones may have lost their geographical orientation, if they had any; but "mature" folks dallying in the same areas must have lost their moral bearing, if they had any.

With your newly found human and Christian ideals, you might be tempted to attach the warning sign "Keep away from adults" to those glossy, smutty magazines, alongside their barcode price tags. I understand your zeal and propensity for heroic crusades. That's typical of converts. But don't dare attach that label! It's an ineffective approach. Besides, the cops might detain you. We live in a "free" world where devils and angels coexist. But you can help change society via a longer route: breaking down structures of sin, uprooting deeply ingrained habits, changing a relativist culture, overcoming rock-bottom ignorance and cleaning up a putrid environment. If you want to re-Christianize the world, begin with yourself by hanging a warning sign in your mind and in your heart. You're not a kid anymore, so you can't put "Keep away from children."

Instead, write something that serves as your guide for the rest of your life: "Keep away from Children of God."

---

[1] St. Josemaría Escrivá, *The Way*, no. 375.

[2] Leo J. Trese, *Human But Holy: Getting To Know God, Yourself and Your Neighbor*. Manila: Sinag-Tala Publishers, Inc., 1999, p. 22.

[3] Peter Kreeft, *Your Questions, God's Answers*. San Francisco: Ignatius Press, 1994, pp. 39-40.

[4] Benedict XVI, *God and the World: A Conversation with Peter Seewald*. San Francisco: Ignatius Press, 2002, p. 89.

[5] *Ibid.*

Chapter Three

STOP, LOOK & LISTEN!

"Stop, Look & Listen!" is a triple warning conspicuous to anybody who crosses a railroad. You can't miss those bold, reflectorized letters. I used to think that those safeguards were overdrawn, a bit exaggerated. There's a watchtower, a traffic light next to it, plus a striped horizontal barrier that's lowered when a locomotive is about to pass. Besides, it blows an ear-piercing horn to announce its impending arrival. The railway itself can't be overlooked. At night a floodlight shines dazzlingly bright. And it takes just two seconds or so to get to the other side, and even less when you're driving fast. So why multiply the palladia?

I thought it was safety overkill until I witnessed a tragic accident involving a mini-bus that was bulldozed by a fast moving train. Two-dozen people died on the spot, gouged out, smashed, pinned down and dragged hundreds of meters. I haven't seen anything as gory; human limbs and metal fragments were scattered all over the scene. Literally it was "overkill," and all because the bus driver tried foolishly to beat the red light. Imprudence can have a very high cost. He should have learned from the Book of Proverbs: "The prudent man looks where he is going." (Prov 14:15)

Street-Smart Virtue

A locomotive is a self-propelled vehicle running on rails, in contrast to the horse-drawn carriages of old. Forced as the analogy may be, the human person, too, is an autonomous and self-determining individual. We're not puppets or marionettes pulled by strings in order to move. We are conscious. We make choices. We take initiatives. We opt for one thing or another. In fact we hate being told always what to do and what not. There's in each of us an interior space, a zone of freedom characteristic of human dignity.[1] Being able to act freely gives us depth and identity. It's my decision, I wanted it that way, I chose so, I take responsibility for that, I know what I'm doing and I can handle this.

But do we always do the right thing? How come people make wrong choices? Ill-advised moves? Stupid decisions? Poor judgments? Fatal steps? Terrible mistakes? For the most part, it's because we lack a good set of criteria of action or principles to live by. Perhaps we don't have a good grasp of the real situation. Or we have developed bad habits. It's time to ponder and get to the bottom of things. We need to have a clear goal in life and a benchmark of moral conduct. Prudence allows us to make sound judgments. Anything you decide on, make sure you know the odds. Weigh your options! Seek sound advice! Learn from the past! It pays to "Stop, Look and Listen"—to be prudent in every crossroad of daily life.

Prudence, in a nutshell, is right reason in action (*recta ratio agibilium*), if we take the classical definition of the Greek philosopher Aristotle. It's the most basic trait of a person who tries to live a good life. By "good" we mean upright, not happy-go-lucky and comfort-loving. A prudent man discerns what's truly good in every circumstance and picks the suitable means to do it. He decides well in the here and now of daily life. The virtue is aptly called the "street-smart" element of human moral behavior, very important in forming our character and guiding our conduct.

Life is a series of choices. When we reach the age of reason, we begin to use our freedom non-stop in manifold and contingent situations. That covers practically all our waking hours. In a sense, we are whom we choose to be. We shape our lives, map out our future and mold our own character. The films we opt to watch, the friends we spend time with, the places we hang out in, the books we pick to read, the websites we click on, the food we eat, the career we pursue, the woman or man we marry, and the state of life we embrace. Since life offers a wide range of possibilities, we had better know how to choose well. This requires a good blend of learning and experience.

Children, because of their inexperience, cannot generally be called "prudent." Little boys and girls may be cute and charming, but they have yet to be initiated in rational thinking, in the school of virtues. They act by gut-feel. They behave by puerile instinct. If we see a child scribbling on the wall or smudging his face with ketchup or playing with a piece of broken glass, we don't ask why he so behaves. But if a grown up person does these, we would conclude that he's nuts. Character formation, though, doesn't come with age. It is acquired. No wonder we see so many people mature in age, but infantile in behavior. Similarly there are young people who are wise, thanks to virtues they've acquired early on.

I recall the protagonist in Evelyn Vaugh's short story, *Too Much Tolerance*. The main character was a dewy-eyed man who regarded everyone as a "jolly good fellow." One of his friends ran off with his wife. Another stole his inheritance. He might have been a nice person but he could not distinguish the good from the bad. So he allowed himself to be fooled. He was a miserable man, estranged from his wife and son, forced to sell sewing machines door-to-door in Africa. Too much tolerance is wretched imprudence.

Colloquially the term "prudent" connotes being "sly" or "timid." It's often used to describe a fellow who puts on a false front, engages in cloak-and-dagger activities or is ineptly tentative, naïve and wishy-washy. But in fact the contrary is true. Guided by the judgment of conscience, the prudent person acts in a measured way so as to avoid falling into either extreme: being heedless and indiscreet on the one hand, or spineless and irresolute on the other. Prudence guides us in applying moral principles to concrete cases and overcoming doubts as to what is truly harmful or beneficial. Prudence sets rules on other virtues. Not without reason is it called *auriga virtutum* (the charioteer of virtues).[2]

A scriptural passage (Rom 8:5-8) speaks of true and false prudence. The prudence of the flesh is deceitful, manipulative and selfish. It's a sickness of the soul that leads one to take advantage of others, driven by worldly desires. Carnal prudence employs chicaneries to satisfy one's wishes. A person of false prudence is double-faced in his dealings, dishonest in his words, disloyal to his commitments. He sets his heart on worthless things and makes earthly goods his chief reason for existence.[3] True prudence, on the other hand, is borne of a good spirit. He who possesses this virtue is perceptive, ingenious and responsible. Gifted with a capacity to understand people, things and events in their true light, the prudent man thinks straight and acts accordingly. For a Christian, this natural virtue is buttressed, so to speak, by a supernatural prudence infused by the Holy Spirit through which the person, illumined by faith and moved by charity, determines the means to attain his final end: eternal life.

Stop, Look & Listen!

Stop! We're always busy and tied up, rushing here and there. Activism leaves little room for reflection. Decisions are hastily made. We rely on intuition. Things aren't weighed properly. So stop, take time out to pause and ponder! Be still and quiet! Silence and solitude foster wise decisions. We need to beat our brains out if we want a sure step on a crucial matter. Form the habit of deep thinking. Then we begin to see problems in a new light. Clear ideas flood in. There's order in our thoughts. We attain a mature outlook. We develop a keener vision, a deeper perspective.

Passions can eclipse our mind and weaken our will, so we need to check our motives and be composed when making a decision. When we're very upset with someone, it's not the best moment to point out his fault, else we might let slip scathing words, only to regret them later on. "We must try to keep our peace, even if only so as to act intelligently, since the man who remains calm is able to think, to study the pros and cons, to examine judiciously the outcome of the actions he is about to undertake."[4]

Look! Be formed and informed! Try to acquire moral criteria that can guide you through life's vicissitudes. Wise decisions presuppose knowledge of the reality on two levels: the principles of reason and the concrete, down-to-earth realities. We can only decide well if we know things well. The truth conditions our mind. People often fumble and stumble due to ignorance. Bereft of ethical compass and doctrinal points of reference, they're at the mercy of pressures both from without (fads, opinions, polls and ideologies) and from within (pride, greed, lust, anger, gluttony, envy and sloth).

More than once I've overheard this remark: "Sorry if I hurt you, but I didn't mean to" or "I did everything in good faith anyway." Yes, but it isn't enough to mean well. We've got to do the right thing. We thus need to know what's right and wrong, the good to be desired and the evil to be avoided. We can be considered prudent if we act in a reasonable way, following our natural conscience to handle this or that situation.[5]

Sometimes we're at a loss as to the best way to resolve a question. We're blank. One course of action may be just as good as another, or just as risky. Such a dilemma can be agonizing. It's difficult to make a choice, but still we've got to decide. Prudence strikes a delicate balance between grave alternatives.

A controversial play, *The Deputy*, premiered in Berlin in 1963 and was soon translated into English and reached Broadway in New York City. The playwright, Rolf Hochhuth, portrayed Pope Pius XII as a "cowardly" leader for his alleged "silence" amidst the Nazi persecution of the Jews during the Second World War. Had the Roman Pontiff been openly outspoken against the Holocaust, Hochhuth argued, millions of lives would have been saved.

The New York Times found the play too severe in its indictment and the "historical facts" it cited to be disputable. Another magazine, *America*, denounced *The Deputy* as an "an atrocious calumny against the memory of a good and courageous world leader occupying the Chair of Peter during one of the great crises of humanity." Jewish historian Pinchus Lapide responded with a book, *Three Popes and the Jews*, in which he documented how eight hundred thousand Jews survived the Nazi horrors thanks to the intervention and humanitarian efforts of Pius XII.

The Pope might have been restrained, but he was not silent or inactive. It was a calculated reserve to avoid brutal retaliation, as had happened in Holland. In April 1942 the Dutch Catholic bishops issued a letter denouncing Nazi tyranny. The move, heroic as it was, swiftly backfired. The Nazis herded Catholic religious of Jewish origin to the gas chambers of Auschwitz. Among the victims was St. Edith Stein, a Carmelite nun, philosopher and mystic.

Pius XII knew too well what was at stake if he chose to face *overtly* Hitler's killing machine. Circumstances forced him to work surreptitiously. The Vatican forged thousands of documents especially in Southern France to facilitate the escape of thousands of Jews. Nearly every Catholic convent in Europe was hiding Jews. The Pope dispatched nuncios to German-occupied territories to use diplomatic muscle to lessen the victims' sufferings.[6]

The Holy Father acted with prudence to handle an imbroglio. Had he lambasted the pogroms aggressively, he would have met high-handed reprisals and more blood would have been spilt. A more discreet approach was the way to save more lives. Difficult cases like this requires *gnome*—higher judgment, acute perspicacity and extraordinary insight.[7] Pius XII adorned a dark period in history with shining wisdom.

Listen! Seek counsel! Two or three heads are better than one. Even the most brilliant minds aren't self-sufficient. We all need guidance. Every head of state has a team of advisers. Olympic athletes follow their coach. Business tycoons hire consultants. Even the Pope has a spiritual director. Why should we do less when we're trying to settle an important matter? Surely you've got friends with experiences to share, or mature folks who can give useful advice. Don't rely on a hit-and-miss approach, typical of know-it-all fellows going solo on the wings of pride. Pay heed to the words of the wise! And be ready to hear what you don't want to hear but should. Flatterers and yes-men don't help you, only the forthright ones.[8] Above all, consider God's inputs; pray about your plans and anything that weighs on you. Listen to the whisper of the Holy Spirit, who is the best counselor.

Saint Thomas Aquinas considered *docilitas* (docility) to counsel as an integral part of the virtue of prudence. So many people fail because they turn a deaf ear to the truth. Sometimes we're quick to brush aside the suggestions of others, when a little hint from the back row could be the key to solve an issue. It pays to be flexible and open-minded. Get ready to change plans if need be! To be docile, though, is not to pass the buck to others. Yours is the decision and you take responsibility for that.

Check the "relationship status" of your Facebook friends. Many people write "complicated" just to fill up the blank space or ward off snoopy eyes. But some are really entangled in muddled affairs. Here's one example. A young lady working for a bank often went to the gym for regular workouts after office hours. There she met a professional fitness instructor who guided her through a strict physical regimen. He laid out a training program that involved developing a shapely body, boosting aerobic strength, toning up muscles, etc. She was excited. They exchanged SMS to coordinate a schedule. Just five days later he began to show keen interest in her personal life. She thought he was handsome. They felt comfortable with each other. After training sessions they would dine out and hang around. Her older brother stepped in: "You better stay away from a man you barely know. That guy has a bad reputation." "We're just friends," she protested. "He's a fitness guru. I know what I'm doing." "Oh yeah, good luck!" he retorted. But she couldn't keep him off her mind. He started asking for money and she couldn't say no. How could she, when infatuation had blinded her? Next thing she knew she was pregnant. The relationship turned sour when she found out that two other women in the same gym were also romantically involved with the man. Worse, he vanished from the scene, leaving her with a shattered life. She knocked on the door of her brother's apartment and when he opened, she broke down in tears—inconsolably. "I told you so. Don't worry sis, we'll help you through this."

Memoria and *Solertia*

A wise move, a prudent action, involves three steps: deliberation, judgment and action. Before we plunge into something, we better mull it over, especially if it's a serious matter. You don't just sign a contract without knowing its terms and conditions. Common sense tells you not to open your door to a stranger just because he seems so nice. It's not wise to rely on a pediatrician to treat your acute respiratory problems. Would you let your teenage child go on a 3-day camping with a group you don't really know? Would you drive a rickety car along the motorway? To act in these cases without due consideration is thoughtlessness.

Past experiences offer valuable lessons. *Memoria* (memory) or the remembrance of what has gone before is a great aid when making decisions. The times we succeeded or bungled. History is an open book. We can understand well the present if we know the past. We need not reinvent the wheel. If you think you've got a fantastic idea, chances are it's not original; many others have thought about it better and long before you. It's a requirement of prudence to recall where we or other people made the wrong turn so as not to fall into the same pit. Or how they succeeded so we can follow in their footsteps. Read! Do a bit of research! Study! Ask around!

Sometimes we need to make a quick decision. A sudden twist of circumstance can put us on the spot and there's not much time to dwell on a very urgent matter. *Solertia* (sagacity) is the technical term in moral theology that refers to the ability to form clear-sighted judgment in the face of the unexpected.[9] A doctor is about to perform a coronary surgery when the patient's blood sugar level shoots up. A plane running low on fuel is radioed by the control tower to hover for a while before landing due to runway traffic. Hours before his much-awaited wedding my brother got the tragic news that our dad had just passed away. These are different situations, but they all pose a common challenge: think and decide fast.

Pressed to make up one's mind in an instant, you may hit it right with a spur-of-the-moment decision using sheer impulse. That's good luck, not prudence. Clear-headed individuals are able to think and act well in a snap, accustomed as they are to making correct judgments.

Prudent men and women are circumspect and cautious: they are able to see the connection of various circumstances even as they look out for pitfalls and seek to minimize whatever adverse effects may result. Above all, they have foresight. Nobody knows the future, but we can somehow anticipate the turn of events with a forward-looking mind. If it's plain common sense to plan things ahead and not get caught unawares, prudence allows us even more to order the means at our disposal so we may attain our goals.

Robert Vanderpoel, a renowned financial journalist of the *Chicago Sun-Times* observed, "The most successful businessman is the man who holds onto the old just as long as it is good, and grabs the new just as soon as it is better." Being shrewd and quick-witted are necessary qualities for any entrepreneur. However, this is technical prudence or skill, not a moral virtue. We may possess rare business acumen (or artistic talent) and yet lack integrity, in the same way that we can be right-minded, but inept at making business deals (or art crafts).[10]

Knowing what to do is one thing, doing it is another. Once we've figured out a problem, we must act promptly. It's pointless to linger unnecessarily. Some people are trapped in a cycle of decision and indecision.

Inconstancy paralyzes them. At times we may have to change our mind especially if new data surface or circumstances change. But this has nothing to do with fickle-mindedness. When a person is irresolute, his "judgment tumbles into futility instead of pouring usefully into the finality of a decision."[11] Until we carry out our good plans, it can't really be said that we have acted prudently in a given instance. The command of the will to execute and set things in motion is the most important element of prudence, since this virtue is a habit of the practical (not theoretical) intellect.[12] Action, we say, speaks more than words.

Perhaps the fear of making a wrong move holds us back. Sheer sloth may also be the culprit. We put things off and make other people wait. But inaction can be worse than an imperfect decision. It can spoil a whole project and chip away at one's credibility. Prudence isn't just about doing the right thing; it also means doing them at the right moment. If we want to accomplish something, then get the ball rolling! Stick to your decision even if only to help you develop a purposeful mind! It sounds funny but have you experienced dining with your friends in a restaurant and no one knows what to order? The clock is ticking, you're all hungry and the waiter is kept on hold. Indecision can delay simple things like this. But of course, it affects more serious things in life when we decide, for example, on which job to take, career path to follow, place to dwell, business to invest in or insurance plan to adopt. My relatives couldn't even agree on whether to cremate or bury their grandpa. He would have arisen and intervened if he could, just to settle the dispute.

The virtue of prudence is especially important for authorities because their decisions have a wide impact:

a company executive, a military general, a bishop or a cabinet minister. Their voices carry a certain weight. Whatever they say or do can have an indeterminate chain effect down the line. On a smaller scale, a father, too, has to have practical wisdom in running his household. So with the case of a school principal, ship captain, editor-in-chief and anyone else with clout. In fact, everyone's actions, good or evil, have repercussions beyond what we could imagine.

Somehow prudence can't be easily passed on to others. It is present in all the virtues and the prudent man can scarcely explain how he practices it. He simply has it by force of habit. Quite naturally he is sensible and far-sighted, never acting carelessly. Prudence is acquired with time. As we grow up we get more experience in life, we understand a lot of things without anyone teaching us. This knowledge is partly innate, partly earned.

Classical Roots

In classical Rome *sapientia* was the word used to describe both theoretical and practical wisdom. *Prudentia* was not clearly defined as a philosophical concept before Cicero's time. This word is a contraction of *providentia* (foresight) and at first it referred mainly to actions with legal effects. Hence, the technical term *iuris prudentia* (legal expertise) and its association with jurists.

The word *prudentia* is seldom found in early Latin. Its meaning evolved from the practice of a person who is described as *prudens*. What is more common is its opposite, the adjective *imprudens*, usually applied to young lovers in a comedy who act rashly, ignoring the legal consequences of their actions. Against this backdrop, *prudentia* came to refer to the quality of an older person with practical experience and understanding of the law, able to discern right and wrong, inclined to do what is proper and takes responsibility for his own actions. The term is also applied to speech, such that a prudent person knows when to speak and when to be quiet. In Roman history, a certain Cato the Elder mentioned a boy named Papirius Praetextatus, who didn't reveal to his mother the topics discussed in the Senate, illustrating his *prudentia*. For displaying this virtue, he was awarded the name Praetextatus that referred to the toga worn by Rome's senior magistrates.[13]

Since the Greek and Roman periods, the virtue of prudence has been symbolized by a woman carrying an arrow (signifying strength of purpose), a mirror (for seeing the world and oneself as one really is) and a serpent (for wisdom). Prudence comes first among the four cardinal virtues and has the unique role of combining the past (memorial), the present (intelligential) and the future (providential).

> Finally, brethren, whatever is true, whatever is honorable, whatever is just, whatever is pure, whatever is lovely, whatever is gracious, if there is any excellence, if there is anything worthy of praise, think about these things. (Phil 4:8)

Just how important is the virtue of prudence? Jesus told his disciples: "Behold, I send you out as sheep in the midst of wolves; so be wise as serpents and innocent as doves." (Mt 10:16) He warned them to be careful because the task at hand involved hazards, oppositions, even the risk of death. If they were too naïve, the world would devour them. And yet they had to be meek and humble as they went around preaching the Gospel. The message was pretty clear: "Don't fool people, but don't be fooled either; walk on the tightrope balance of prudence!" These words are also addressed to us, but couched in different terms: "*Stop, Look and Listen!*"

---

[1] Juan Luis Lorda, *The Virtues of Holiness: The Basics of Spiritual Struggle*. New York: Scepter Publishers, 2010, p. 49.

[2] *Catechism of the Catholic Church*, no. 1806.

[3] St. Thomas Aquinas, *Summa Theologiae*, IIa-IIae, q. 55, a. 1.

[4] St. Josemaría Escrivá, *Friends of God*, no. 79.

[5] Josef Pieper, *The Four Cardinal Virtues*. Indiana: University of Notre Dame Press, 1966, pp. 10-11.

[6] Donald De Marco, *The Many Faces of Virtue*. Ohio: Emmaus Road Publishing, 2000, pp. 219-221.

[7] Celestine Bittle, *Man and Morals*. Milwaukee: The Bruce Publishing Company, 1950, p. 256.

[8] Lorda, *op. cit.*, p. 52.

[9] Pieper, *op. cit.*, p. 13.

[10] Bittle, *op. cit.*, p. 255.

[11] Pieper, *op. cit.*, p. 13.

[12] Bittle, *op. cit.*, p. 255.

[13] Robert Hariman (ed.), *Prudence: Classical Virtue, Postmodern Practice*. Philadelphia: Penn State University Press, 2003, p. 37.

Chapter Four

PAY AS YOU ORDER

Pay as you order is a typical policy of restaurants where you just walk in, order food and drink, pay and then sit down to enjoy a hearty meal. So with fast food joints, quick orders, Burger-Machine food vans in a little corner, a hole in the wall food counter for people on the go. Quite different are those fine dining restaurants with crisp tablecloths, impeccable napkins and waiters in tuxedos serving prized patrons. An attendant comes when you're ready to bill out. But whether you queue with your food tray in a self-service cafeteria to pay the cashier or call on the waiter to swipe your credit card, it's all basically the same—you pay for your order.

That's the crux of the matter: Pay up! Hand in the amount that is due! It's actually common sense but in a world marred by deceit and corruption, people had better be prodded to fulfill their obligations of justice even if the amount involved is a pittance. We all know how much it hurts to be swindled and treated unfairly. It's not so much the lost benefits that matter; it's the insult against our personal honor. This has no price. That's why we feel indignant when someone tries to do us wrong. Even in simple things like lining up, you would probably rile up if a fellow squeezes himself in front of you in a queue.

On the other hand, we don't employ fraud just to get what we want, because it's debasing. An honest guy won't cheat in a school test, sports competition, or business deal but would follow the rules of fair play. He would rather settle for less than stain his soul.

Pay as you order in fact refers to any "liability" in our day-to-day life. It can be to return what you borrow, settle your account, do well the job you're paid to do, honor your contract, pitch in your share, report punctually or flush the toilet. If we are remiss in our "debts" or duties, we had better be ready to suffer the consequence. Of course we can be on either side of the equation, the debtor or the indebted.

We're not alone in the world and we don't own it. Nobody has a monopoly of rights and privileges. Let's learn to share the earth's goods with our fellowmen. It pays to respect other people's rights and fulfill our obligations earnestly. We are social by nature and justice is absolutely essential in social relations. Do you want to get along well with other people? Start by being fair! Pay for what you should! It must sink deep into our minds that whatever belongs to our neighbor is theirs, in the same way that we expect them to respect what's truly ours. Fair treatment of others is a mark of true nobility.

Paperclip Integrity

Justice is defined by the classics in a single phrase: *suum cuique* or "to each his own." From the ancient times this notion was upheld by Plato, Aristotle, Cicero,

Ambrose, Augustine and especially the Roman law,[1] and became the patrimony of Western legal tradition. A more precise concept is found in Justinian's *Corpus Juris Civilis*: "Justice is a habit whereby a man renders to each one his due with constant and perpetual will."[2] Its root is the Latin term *ius* which means "right." Hence, justice seeks to establish what is right, to put order and equality. Right implies some debt, something owed, an obligation that needs to be met or fulfilled by someone. A just man is one who always settles anything owed, does what's supposed to be done and sets things right (*ius*).[3] A just state of affairs means that a relation of equality is observed.

Because the world is imperfect and people do bad things, society guarantees individual rights. We thus find in the civil code of every civilized nation variants of the admonition *pay as you order*, but in more precise legal terms and backed by the full force of law.[4] You must have seen an image or statue of a blindfolded woman holding a set of scales in her right hand and a two-edged sword in her left hand. She is *Justitia*, the Roman goddess of justice found in trial courts, halls of justice, faculties of law and legal manuals. The iconography symbolizes the workings of justice where the blindfold stands for objectivity, the scales represent the balancing of arguments, and the two-edged sword signifies the power to enforce justice.[5]

One of the four cardinal moral virtues, justice is basically an inner inclination, an attitude respectful of others' rights. It is a moral disposition, but make no mistake about it. We are considered just or unjust by what we do, not by what we say we do or plan to do. *Per exteriores actus* (through external acts), says St. Thomas Aquinas, men are ordained to one another.[6] I would be held liable even if had I really intended to pay for my order, but owing to sheer forgetfulness, stepped out of the restaurant without settling the bill.

We tend to trust a fellow if we know that he is not the dodgy and shady type, but rather tried-and-true, one who accounts for everything down to the last penny. Justice is not an occasional, on-and-off display of rectitude, but a stable habit like any other moral virtue. A just man acts rather predictably—i.e., reputably. There is maturity of spirit, fair judgment and personal responsibility. He is detached from the love of material things and has good self-control, qualities necessary to combat greed and avarice, the vices that are the root causes of all injustice.

There's a saying that goes: "Every man has his price." Pay enough and you can get anyone to do practically anything you want. I call it a loser's maxim. For all its troubles, the world does not lack men and women of integrity who can't be bought. Conscience, not money, is what guides their conduct.[7]

Whether dealing with a dime or billions of dollars, a paperclip or a large estate, a just person does what he knows in conscience to be fair. Without being fussy and ridiculously meticulous about things, let's call it "paperclip integrity." Because "he who is faithful in very little is also faithful in much; and he who is dishonest in very little is dishonest also in much." (Lk 16:10)

I read in the local papers an inspiring story of a cab driver who returned a clutch bag containing a sizable amount of cash to its owner. The valuables belonged to his passenger who had hurriedly gotten off the cab. As soon as he realized it, our little hero searched the bag for contact numbers and called up at once. In a media interview, the wheelman said it never occurred to him to just keep the money and keep mum. "It's not me, that's not the way I act…I don't keep things that aren't mine."

We humans have a common frail condition: the penchant to possess and get hold of anything we find desirable, even if it's not really ours, even if it's obtained by dubious means, even if it's beyond what's reasonable. We're aghast at how people unconscionably resort to illicit ways of doing things, abuse their authority, obtain undue advantage, break the rules of the game, twist the arm of the law, use underhanded means, exert undue influence, tamper with documents and disregard the truth. Unbridled individualism and selfishness breed injustice. If our world revolved around "me," "mine" and "myself," we would likely step on other people's toes and infringe on their rights.

Some guide points for self-examination might help us acquire a keener sense of justice. Do we report to work on time? Are we honest in money matters? Do we return in good condition the things we borrow? We don't sneak out office supplies for personal use, do we? Do we blurt out words that put others in a bad light or tarnish their good reputation? Are we control-freaks, or do we recognize the due autonomy of people? Do we observe business ethics? Do our clients and customers get their money's worth? Are we guilty of favoritism? Of nepotism? Of discrimination? Hold on! Do we cheat on our spouse? We can lengthen the list of pointers *ad infinitum*, but suffice it to say that justice requires purity of intention and upright conduct in all areas affecting interpersonal relations.

Small acts of self-denial may well help us be a little more just. Ego-tripping is often the culprit behind unfair practices. Being just requires a delicate conscience. It's not the fear of backlash that moves us to act honestly, but the attraction of virtue. Prudent motorists observe speed limits not because speed detectors are in sight or the fine for violation is high, but simply because they are just.

We all know the golden rule: *Do not do unto others what you would not want others do unto you.* Treat people in the same way that you would want them to treat you, that is to say, fairly. Each time we do something, we better be circumspect. We regret the times we have acted thoughtlessly, how we hurt others. Learn the art of harmonious living! Know what's right and wrong in social life, the extent of our duties and limits of our freedom, the sensibilities of those around us.

"Justice" goes to the core of our being. It brings to light our human dignity that is often buried beneath layers of cultural constructs and social conventions, the trappings of confused values characteristic of postmodern society. When the man or the woman next to you has nothing to boast of—no money, no education, no shelter, no clothing, the person still retains his or her human dignity as a child of God, albeit hardly perceptible to the eyes of the world so used to judging the external. That dignity is inalienable and inviolable, what we all have radically in common. That person deserves respect as much as we do. When society and circumstance deprive an individual of everything, what's left is a brother or sister worthy of help; what's exposed is the image of bare humanity, what you and I are at rock bottom, hidden underneath our titles, honors, distinctions, credentials and possessions and yes, under the silk and jeans we wear. Justice brings to the fore our fundamental equality as humans, regardless of race, sex, wealth, culture and religion.

True vs. Bogus Rights

We do well when we claim and defend what is truly ours, be it material goods (e.g., property, title, ownership) or spiritual goods (e.g., honor, dignity, freedom). You don't just cross your arms and do nothing if someone snatches your bag or a person maligns you publicly. Surely you won't keep quiet if your teacher flunks you when you know you did very well in class; or if your salary is withheld for unknown reasons, or if the plumber you hired does a lousy job or you're barred from entering a bistro café simply because of the color of your skin. Even pre-school kids cry foul if someone grabs their toys.

But how do we know what's ours and what belongs to our fellowmen? Broadly speaking, we lay claim to something either because the law bestows it on us (legal rights) or we possess it by nature (natural human rights). The former is acquired, for example, by exchange and contracts (e.g., I can do what I want with whatever I buy; I'm entitled to just compensation for the job I do). The latter is *a priori* and inherent. We possess it because we are humans. We owe to no one on earth the fact that we are free to breathe, speak, eat, learn, worship, work and move around. These are basic human rights, inviolable and inalienable.

That's how ancient Roman law and jurisprudence resolved disputes. The diversity of customs among the inhabitants of the vast Roman Empire required a standard legal approach. To settle the conflict between a Spanish merchant and a French trader, for example, the court applied natural law which is universal and hence, binding to all. Much of the contemporary legal systems of the Western world trace their origins in Roman law.

In the same vein, the United States *Declaration of Independence* (1776) recognizes the "self-evident" truth that "all men are created equal" and "that they are endowed by their Creator with certain unalienable Rights...."⁸ Perhaps the need to protect basic human rights was felt most in the aftermath of the Second World War when mankind was at its worst. In TED Talks, former CNN president Jonathan Klein quoted an Auschwitz survivor as saying that "the Nazi holocaust teaches us that nature, even in its cruelest moments, is benign in comparison with man when he loses his moral compass and his reason." The horrors of that war gave rise to the United Nations Declaration of Human Rights (1948), crafted ostensibly to preclude similar blatant abuses of human rights in the future.

The Greek philosopher Aristotle said that the prevalence of injustice makes clear the meaning of justice, quite in the same way that the chiaroscuro of lights and shadows brings out the main subject in a piece of art. Violence almost always erupts when rights, especially fundamental human rights, are violated. Major world conflicts, political agitations and social unrest flare up for the same reason. History is replete with examples of how people clamor for change in the face of glaring injustices, such as the fight for the abolition of slavery in England, the civil liberty movement in the US and the peace crusade of Mahatma Gandhi in India. Closer to our time, we recall the dismantling of Apartheid in South Africa, the collapse of the Iron Curtain at the end of the cold war, the battle for democracy in Myanmar, the Guantanamo scandal, the Arab Spring uprisings, and Occupy Wall Street Movement, to name a few. These are landmark struggles for human freedom in the face of oppression, popular revolts to reclaim what has been unduly usurped. The major political and social upheavals have a characteristic pattern: the systematic denial of basic human rights by state authorities or occupying power, and the subsequent mass mobilization—peaceful or violent—to overthrow the dominant forces and install a regime of change and equality. It's in the nature of man to defend what is his. If he can't do it now, surely later.

Contemporary society has acquired a more acute sense of justice. There's a heightened awareness of human rights and sensitivity to anything that curtails legitimate freedom. Tolerance has become a byword in schools, hospitals, offices, city squares, markets and the halls of Congress. Young people now grow up with the notion that everybody has a place on planet earth, including the crippled, the unlettered, and the weird. Buildings, public parks and mass transport are now designed so the wheelchair bound invalids can ably move about because they, too, have rightful access to them just like the rest of us. It seems only the unborn children, the most defenseless creatures, are denied the most fundamental right to life, paradoxically in countries that are purportedly champions of human liberty. How come?

Not all rights have the same importance. Some rights are primary, inherent in every person, like the right to life, freedom of speech and the right to the truth. These rights do not change. Other rights are secondary. They vary according to one's circumstance, responsibility or state in life. Voters, employees, artists and students are distinct social groups with different rights that may change across space and time.

The trouble is that in today's world primary rights and secondary rights are often confused and swapped.

Worse, false rights are invented while real ones are suppressed. You can guess the outcome. The "wrongs" are proclaimed as "rights." Evil deeds become the order of the day.[9] This is what happens when the so-called women's "reproductive health right" trumps the right to life of the unborn child via abortion. Or when the "right against discrimination" is used to justify the "right" to same-sex "family" unions. "Rights" get mixed up and messed up. But here's a worse irony: animals like apes, dolphins, dogs and bears are accorded "rights" whereas newborn infants and the handicapped are struck out as non-persons shorn of any rights.[10]

Blame it on excessive egalitarianism, the denial of objective moral truth and the consequent "dictatorship of relativism" that Pope-Emeritus Joseph Ratzinger had warned us of. Justice that is not anchored on natural law and ultimately on God is baloney. Any concept of "right" and "wrong" based merely on legal duty[11] is hollow and feckless. It can't really put order in our community. The denial of objective, transcendent truth would unleash wild, selfish motives that pit people against each other. Each one would impose his ideas. Arbitrary rule and tyranny would reign.[12] When norms of conduct cannot appeal to any authority higher than the inherently fickle and flawed mind of human legislators, what we have is legal positivism, a disease that haunts most justice systems today. Talking about contemporary problems of justice, Dr. Francis Beckwith, an American philosopher, Christian apologist and professor of Church-State Studies at Baylor University, shares the same diagnosis in his timely book entitled *Relativism: Feet Firmly Planted in Mid-Air!*[13]

We live in a world (at least the so-called democratic, free societies) where people fight for their rights and freedom tooth and nail. They defend every inch of their property and dignity. A false report that smears the good name of someone can send the writer to jail for libel. Flirt with a lady colleague and you can be liable for sexual harassment. Doctors may risk prosecution if their patients' condition turns worse. A teacher who spanks a mischievous pupil can be sued for child abuse. Tap a boy on his shoulder and you can reap charges of pedophilia. Recourse to legal means has almost become a collective paranoia especially in Western societies.

Yet injustices continue to hound society. Read the daily news! A big chunk of media headlines uncover malpractices in the form of election fraud, bribery and corruption, business scam, or sensational stories about sexual assault, robbery, murder, abortion, human trafficking, drug syndicates and countless other manifestations of human abuse. These are pandemic moral disorders. We wonder what's happening to the world. Of course the media also carry positive news and inspiring stories. But the shadows often dominate the light. Not everything written about corruption may be true, but for the most part, they carry a grain of truth. Injustice is rampant.

The modern world is marked by a great paradox. It shows itself "at once powerful and weak, capable of the noblest deeds or the foulest; before it lies the path to freedom or to slavery, to progress or retreat, to brotherhood or hatred."[14]

Common Good

Ironically, we see signs of apathy all over. It's already too bad that some people cause others to suffer. But still worse is the fact that many couldn't care less. ABC News conducted a reality check and set up a situation in which a man verbally abused a woman in a public area to see how others would react. Sadly, few people stepped in to stop it. Most of them were women. The rest ignored the spectacle. Perhaps the culprit is rugged individualism, that sickness of free societies that makes one avoid interfering in other people's lives—even if sometimes they have to.[15]

People can be indifferent if they're not directly affected. Or abuse and injustice have become commonplace. Maybe they're too occupied. Or they feel powerless to make any difference. The duty to act for the good of society? Leave it to heroes out there!

> For too many people, justice never goes beyond words and into deeds. Our generation tends to bitch and moan about the problems in society, politics, and the world, but fails to take any action to rectify those injustices beyond slapping a witty bumper sticker on the back of their Honda…Apathy is like a contagious disease that spreads from person to person as each individual gives up the passion to fight the good fight. The truth is that each man has the responsibility to fight for justice in any capacity he can.[16]

Even God suffered injustice in the hands of men. Remember Pilate? He knew deep within that Jesus was innocent. In fact his wife urged him not to tangle with the King of the Jews because he was really a *righteous* man. (Cf. Mt 27:19) But cowardice got the better of him, so he suppressed the truth and steered the wheel of justice towards political convenience, to the "detriment" of Christ. All these would sum up of course to our salvation. But the mock trial and the crucifixion of the Nazarene show us the tremendous evil of injustice. They also show what happens when someone who can do something about injustice chickens out.

The social edifice is ultimately built on the integrity of its individual members, just as structures of evil are but towering piles of personal sins. Dig deep into corruption issues and each case, though it may cover a wide and intricate web of agencies and elements in cahoots with each other, is often traced to a rotten main trunk, usually the top brass who are ravenous wolves in sheep's clothing. Which is why a concerted effort is also needed to clean up a dirty political landscape and decadent culture.

Justice is *conditio sine qua non* for peace, order and stability to reign in any society. It is the linchpin of human progress. Without it society hangs on a precarious balance, doomed to crumble down like a house of cards. Every justice system is a barometer that indicates how developed or primitive is a given society, how stable or fragile is its body politic.

Hence, the virtue of justice is closely bound up with the concept of the common good—the sum total of the conditions of social life that enables men and women to attain their perfection more fully and readily.[17] It calls for social awareness and responsibility, a sense of solidarity and commitment to seek the good of others, more so at a time when the world is becoming a single community dubbed as the global village. The interconnectedness of peoples and cultures, aided by modern technology, calls us all to share in the task of building a civilization of peace and justice. All these have deep implications for the rights and duties of each individual.[18]

Beyond Legal Justice

Very broadly speaking, *justice* covers all virtues and it means "perfection" or "holiness." This is often the meaning applied by the Sacred Scriptures. Abraham, Isaac, Moses and the patriarchs and prophets of old are just in this sense. Saint Joseph, the foster Father of Jesus, was a *just man*. (Cf. Mt 1:19) But as a cardinal virtue the scope of *justice* is more restrictive. It refers to the inclination to render to other people what they have the right to demand from us—life, health, wage, property, reputation and freedom.[19]

The debt of gratitude we owe our donors, patrons and benefactors would fall within this ambit of justice. So too, the obedience and respect our parents deserve. Even the worship due to God as the source of our being and every good thing in us is a matter of justice. It's just fair, we say, to acknowledge and somehow return the favor and blessings we have received.

However, "justice" properly so-called requires three elements: alterity (directed toward another person), exactitude (what is strictly due is quantifiable) and equivalence (what is rendered corresponds to what is due). The precise scope and meaning of "justice" makes it a special moral virtue. Many other virtues resemble "justice" in some way, but they fail to meet entirely its triple requirements. They are annexed, potential parts, cognates or cousins, so to speak, of "justice." Among these are truthfulness, gratitude, generosity, affability, piety, obedience and religion.[20] I am not as duty-bound to smile and courteously greet a friend I meet in the corridor, as I am obliged to pay for the hamburger I ordered.

Piety or "dutifulness" (*pietas* in Latin), to give another example, prods us to obey and respect mom and dad. But piety exceeds the limits of strict justice. Obviously we can't repay our parents enough for all that they've done, their toils and sacrifices for you and me as we grew up. As our way of saying "Thank you," we may shower them with untold gifts, fly them to exotic places, give them the best medical care or stay by their bedside, yet that's no match to their invaluable love as dear parents. We can't speak of real equivalence here.

While living in Rome, I would occasionally dine with a friend at my favorite restaurant near the area where I was doing research. A few beggars, mostly jobless migrants, would trickle in around one in the afternoon. Without much ado, the attendant at the counter would hand them free packed meals. It was a daily routine. Curious, I approached one waiter to ask about it. "Ah, it's our social outreach, feed the poor," he explained. I was impressed.

What we have here, though, is not a strict obligation of justice, but a gesture of solidarity and compassion, borne out of charity. We may call it a corporal work of mercy or social justice (this is natural, not merely legal, justice) if you will, sheer concern for the underprivileged. The paupers of course do not pay for what they receive—there's no equivalence between their greeting *buona sera* and the food doled out to them. Yet they deserve all kinds of help and support. Justice is giving someone what is his; charity is giving him what is mine.

The world is teeming with people hungry for social justice. From Somalia to Bangladesh, from Albania to Papua New Guinea, and yes, from the United States to Germany, in every corner of every continent, there are countless men and women, children and elderly, whose lives are a portrait of poverty, material or moral. The great divide between the rich and the poor is a gaping scandal that calls for urgent action from world leaders and policy makers. Solidarity is not just about sending relief goods and humanitarian aid to victims of tsunamis, hurricanes and earthquakes. Nor is it reduced to Corporate Social Responsibility (CSR) projects very much in vogue in today's corporate world. Social justice is a pressing concern that demands commitment to remedy unjust structures and social inequalities.

Next time you see the signage *pay as you order*, take it as more than just a friendly reminder to customers! Let it ring a bell calling us to act justly in every way. And we will have helped make this world a better place to live.

---

[1] Josef Pieper, *The Four Cardinal Virtues*. Indiana: University of Notre Dame Press, 1966, p. 44.

[2] Russell Kirk, *The Meaning of Justice*. The Heritage Foundation Leadership for America, in http://www.heritage.org/research/lecture/the-meaning-of-justice.

[3] Doug Macmanaman, *The Virtue of Justice*, in http://catholiceducation.org/articles/education/ed0285.html.

[4] "Every person must…act with justice, give everyone his due and observe honesty and good faith." He who "willfully…causes damage, loss or injury to another in a manner contrary to morals, good customs or public policy…or acquires something at the expense of another person, shall… indemnify or compensate the latter…." Chapter 2, Articles 19-22, *Civil Code of the Philippines*. Comparable provisions are found in the civil codes of many other countries.

[5] Michael Hayes, *The virtue of justice: Ad alterum*, in http://thepastoralreview.org/index.php/issues/past-issues/36-

november-december-2012/61-the-virtue-of-justice-ad-alterum.

[6] St. Thomas Aquinas, *Summa Theologica*, I, II, q. 100, a. 2.

[7] Juan Luis Lorda, *The Virtues of Holiness: The Basics of Spiritual Struggle*. New York: Scepter Publishers, 2010, p. 54.

[8] http://www.archives.gov/exhibits/charters/declaration_transcript.html.

[9] Bishop Thomas Olmsted, *The Virtue of Justice*, in http://www.catholicculture.org/culture/library/view.

[10] Charles Rice, *50 Questions on the Natural Law*. San Francisco: Ignatius Press, 1993. Reprinted in the Philippines by National Bookstore, Inc., and Theological Centrum, Manila, 1996, pp. 63-65.

[11] Anscombe, credited for reviving *Virtue Ethics* in mid-20th century with his book *Modern Moral Philosophy* (1958), maintained that ethics would not have any real foundation without belief in the Divine legislator. Notions like "right" and "wrong" do not have meaning unless God is put into the picture. Cf. Marzieh Zadequi, *Justice as a Virtue of the Soul*, in http://messageofthaqalayn.com/justice.pdf, pp. 104-105.

[12] St. John Paul II, *Centesimus Annus* (1991), no. 44.

[13] He is co-authored by Gregory Koukl.

[14] Second Vatican Council, *Gaudium et spes* (1965), no. 9.

[15] Brett McKay and Kate McKay, *The Virtuous Life: Justice*, in http://www.artofmanliness.com/2008/04/20/the-virtuous-life-justice/ The Virtuous Life: Justice

[16] *Ibid.*

[17] Second Vatican Council, *Gaudium et spes* (1965), no. 26.

[18] As a summary of principles, *General Ethics* classifies *Justice* into *Legal* or *General* (regulates the actions of individuals vis-à-vis the community where they belong and inclines each one to render to society its due for the sake of the common

good) and *Particular justice* (regulates the actions of individuals in relation to others and inclines him to give them what's theirs). *Particular justice* can be *commutative* (orders the dealings between individuals) or *distributive* (orders the dealings of society towards its members). *Commutative justice* embodies the concept of justice more perfectly because it implies the distinction and separation between persons and it demands arithmetical equivalence, article for article, penny for penny or its equivalent, according to strict valuation. When injustice is done, only *commutative justice* imposes the obligation of restitution (i.e., restore the damage, compensate the loss, redress the grievance). Celestine Bittle, *Man and Morals*. Milwaukee: The Bruce Publishing Company, 1950, pp. 257-258. See also Pieper, *op. cit.*, pp. 70-75.

[19] Bittle, *op. cit.*, p. 257.

[20] *Ibid.*, pp. 261-262.

CHAPTER FIVE

BREAK GLASS IN CASE OF EMERGENCY

A fundamental rule of safety when you first enter a building—theater, hotel, convention center or shopping mall—is to spot the emergency exit. It is not being paranoid about accidents, but it pays to be prudent so you won't be caught off guard in any eventuality.

In corridors, foyers and staircases one may find a fire extinguisher or a long hose reel perched in a niche on the wall, encased in transparent glass on which is written in bold, red letters: *Break Glass in Case of Emergency!* Not with bare hands of course, but there's a tiny hammer or ax next to the box. If it's a portable device, it carries clear instructions: Hold upright. Pull ring pin. Stand back 10 feet. Aim at base of fire. Squeeze lever. Sweep side to side.

It's pretty easy to use this security mechanism, but it takes a lion's heart to handle a crisis situation. One has to have the guts to act swiftly. It's not for the weak-kneed and fainthearted. Likewise, when you board a plane and sit next to the emergency exit, a flight attendant politely checks if you're really up to it.

What if you're at the zero hour and people are in a panic. Can you think straight and do what must be done? It's tempting perhaps to just run for one's life. Remember the fallen heroes of 9/11? A band of firemen, medics and clergy rushed into the Twin Towers in a dramatic attempt to rescue thousands of people trapped inside. They staked their lives in response to a call of duty. Moments later, they were all buried under the rubble and went down the annals of history as paragons of patriotism.

Brave It Out!

Have you ever done a brave or heroic act? Perhaps there just wasn't an opportunity to show your mettle. Be that as it may, would you do what's right even if it involved risks or demanded sacrifice? A firm character is needed not only during crunch time. It is just as important in the humdrum of daily life. Fortitude sees things through when a problem requires quick, decisive action or a slow, painstaking effort; when it calls for a supreme heroic act or a little deed of duty. Fortitude is what emboldens the soldiers to be in the thick of the battle; but it's also what prods us to wake up on the dot to start a busy day. Whether it's a question of diffusing a time bomb or finishing a thesis, swallowing a bitter pill or tilling the land, correcting a friend or raising a big family, one needs the virtue of fortitude.

Life is tough. Many times our courage and endurance are put to test. We live in an imperfect world. That means a rendezvous with the cross sooner or later. It takes a good dose of fortitude to face up to life's vicissitudes. How we wish things were easy, that circumstances worked in our favor! We make the best of plans. But there are always hitches. We hope for a happy turn of events. But we often meet disappointments. Finances. Romance. Career. Health. Studies. Recreation. You name it! They're almost always a mix of laughter and tears, joys and sorrows. For some, more of the latter. We're not sowing seeds of pessimism here; just opening our eyes to reality. Your own story perhaps is testimony enough of how harsh life can be.

No wonder then that many people are afraid of life. They dread its complications. Many a man recoil and cringe when confronted with challenges of all kinds. There's something that lurks in the mind of the tremulous: "What if…?" "What if I fail?" "What if it doesn't work?" "What if we run short?" And countless other "What ifs" that hold him back from pursuing his aims. Sometimes his fears are baseless, purely imaginary. The fear of having fears paralyzes him. If the obstacles are real, he shrinks all the more. He gives up at the slightest difficulty. That's why a person wanting in fortitude hardly gets anything well done. He settles for the minimum. He seeks the easy way out. He is afraid to commit. He makes short cuts. He lowers the demands. He balks at whatever implies sweat. He runs away from responsibility. He is spineless.

We all have fears. Who doesn't? Even the finest men-at-arms tremble amidst a cross fire. The best pilots have their share of fright before an intense turbulence. Seasoned swimmers and divers can get nervous when the undertow runs strong. These are rare, one might say. But in most other life situations, our moral stamina is also put to test. A salesman may dread his inability to meet the sales target. A student may develop a cold sweat in front of a panel of examiners. A pregnant woman can get anxious about birth pangs as she is wheeled to the maternity ward. A boy can be afraid to tell mom and dad the truth about his bruises. My friend even walked out minutes into watching a horror film, *The Exorcist*. And so everybody else has a share of fears and apprehensions. Somehow we can't really get over that childhood experience of being afraid of the dark. It's normal. It's human.

But we need to overcome our fears in one way or another. Or else we get stuck, like a car buried deep in the mud. We must slug it out even when the going gets rough. Somebody has to *break the glass* and it's got to be you! Fortitude is precisely the virtue that keeps us firm in our resolve to seek what's good in spite of the hardships.[1] Life's journey is full of stumbling blocks, but these are hurdled only by the strong. Our generation often resorts to antidepressants and sedatives as a quick-fix, stop-gap approach to handle pressures, fears and anxieties. But *Prozac* doesn't get to the bottom of the problem. There's really nothing like the inner strength of fortitude.

We admire the person who can hack what others give up on. The kid who chases the stray mouse in the classroom that horrifies the girls is the little hero of the batch. We take our hats off to the man who dares to scale a treacherous mountain peak or penetrate a deep and narrow cavern. Passengers applaud the pilot who successfully lands the plane amidst stormy weather. The cancer patient who serenely bears the throes of terminal ailment inspires us, too, to be brave. So does the working mother who juggles the responsibilities of family life and a full time job. We give her two thumbs up. The whistle blower in a corruption scandal may risk losing his position or even his life, but he is honored for exposing the crooks. And the one who breaks the glass in case of emergency to save lives. They all share one laudable quality: fortitude.

Obverse of Weakness

Paradoxically, only the vulnerable can be brave. Strange as it may sound to you, no one can be courageous except he or she who is prone to injury. The virtue of fortitude is alien to angels (pure spirits) because they're impregnable. Now imagine that Superman or Ironman isn't just a sci-fi fantasy, but real and invincible! He, too, doesn't have to be brave. Nor can he be, if he's always unscathed.

The virtue of fortitude thus implies some degree of fragility. Of all creatures, only the humans can be strong (i.e., display courage) because we're the only beings on earth liable to suffering.[2] Being brave doesn't mean the lack of fear. It means being able to overcome fear, to conquer fright as a natural reaction to dangers. Fortitude arms us with the strength to boldly face the obstacles to our goal. It's readiness to fall in the battle that makes us great.

While living in Italy, my right knee was operated on due to a soccer injury. The surgery went well, but a few days later my knee became swollen. The doctor had to suction fluids out. Holding a huge syringe, he asked: "Do you want anesthesia? We don't usually apply that to toughies." I was put on the spot and blurted out: "No worries, Doc. I have a high threshold for pain." Pride made me say that, not courage. When he learned that I liked to paint using watercolor, he told me that he, too, liked to sketch as pastime and would go outdoors to paint ancient Roman ruins like the Colosseum. Just there and then he pierced my knee with a needle almost the size of a fruit juice straw. I screamed in agony. He told me to come back the next day for another session. I never did.

Fortitude also points to the reality of evil, that is, anything that threatens the good we seek to attain. We need not be daring if nobody or nothing ever stands in our way. Life sails on smoothly. We take everything in stride. But we need to muster strength when we meet roadblocks. We must be tough when we're up against a formidable challenge. Only if we are armed with fortitude can we fight our way through. Problems, they say, create opportunities. The opportunity, above all, to be manly. "Brave men and women (as well as cowardly men and women) are not born that way; they become that way through their acts."[3]

> Fortitude is a certain strength of the will to overcome the fear of effort and of difficulties. The person with fortitude is one who perseveres in doing what his conscience tells him he ought to do…The strong man will at times suffer, but he stands firm; he may be driven to tears, but he will brush them aside. When difficulties come thick and fast, he does not bend before them.[4]

The stories that inspire us most are not those of people who won the jackpot in lotteries and then spent the rest of their lives as couch potatoes. Nor are we really edified by the memoirs of people whose political and financial clout came by way of inheritance. The truly inspiring stories are about those who worked their way up from humble beginnings, those who succeeded by dint of sacrifice, by sheer determination.[5]

Without fortitude we won't get anywhere in life. *A cat in gloves catches no mice.* Failure is what you get from over-caution or false prudence (pussyfooting). If we want to advance, we've got to be ready to take risks and launch out, come what may. We may hesitate for a moment, weigh our chances, but it pays to cross the Rubicon.[6] That said, fortitude is not to be mistaken for presumptuous boldness. It's foolishness to unduly put oneself in grave hazards. If the timorous lacks courage, the reckless has, in a manner of speaking, a bit "too much" of it. He is rashly daring. It's hardly a virtue. The Miriam-Webster dictionary says it's "a madcap scheme to go over Niagara falls in a barrel."

To be strong is not to ignore the real dangers. The brave person is well aware of them and is not exempt from sensations of fear.[7] But he conquers fright to move ahead because *vale la pena* (it's worth the pain). Courage, not false optimism, is what impels him to act despite the perils. If temperance bridles our tendency to overindulge in pleasurable things (eating, sex, comfort, TV, gadgets, internet, physical wellness, etc.), fortitude, on the other hand, firms up our disposition to do what needs doing despite weariness, difficulty or pain (work, studies, family duties, medication, commitment, fraternal correction, telling the truth, fighting for justice, etc.). The former restrains us from going too far, the latter pushes us to avoid falling short. One tames our love of comfort, the other propels us to face the difficulties squarely. Temperance and fortitude are two sides of the same coin.

Fight to Win

Human life is a combat. We're constantly at war. Not that we quarrel with friends and neighbor but we need to wage war because something gets in the way of our aspirations. It can be anything or anyone that derails our plans or complicates our life. Sometimes it's outside of us, like heavy traffic or false accusations; we have to grapple with a harsh environment. But one can also be stymied by inner troubles like cowardice, timidity or sloth. Often the enemy within is harder to beat than the enemy without.

We shouldn't just give up. Fight it out! Endurance, which is a potential part of fortitude, gives us an iron will to shun any spirit of compromise. We hang on especially if we're doing the right thing. And it makes sense to put up a struggle if we know we stand a chance to win. Thus, while fortitude implies vulnerability, it also suggests our ability to succeed. God won't allow anyone of goodwill to be tested beyond his strength.[8] The human spirit can be unstinting and unbending in the pursuit of one's ideals. Our body may suffer fatigue and wounds, but no earthly good can quash the human will, mind and heart because they're made for no less than the Infinite.

> "Man gains…dignity when, ridding himself of all slavery to the passions, he presses forward to his goal by freely choosing what is good and, by his diligence and skill, effectively secures for himself the means suited to this end."[9]

But left to himself, even the strong man cannot possibly withstand severe trials. Sheer human power often fails. The Holy Spirit comes to the rescue with the infused virtue of fortitude which acts not simply in the light of natural reason, but that of faith. "Be watchful! Your adversary the devil prowls around like a roaring lion, seeking someone to devour. Resist him, *fortes in fide*—firm in your faith." (1 Pt 5:8) This supernatural fortitude is like a power booster that enables mere mortals to calmly bear agonizing pains. We are awed by the accounts of Christian martyrs who braved the gallows, furnace, beasts, swords in defense of their faith. No, they did not scorn life; they loved to live and do good. But forced to choose between extremes, they opted to shed their blood rather than apostatize.

Stephen was stoned to death. Perpetua was pierced to the bones. Sebastian was peppered with arrows. Joan of Arc was burnt at the stake. Maximilian Kolbe was starved to death. They and countless other martyrs prayed for and/or aided their executioners do a good job. They overcame the greatest evil—death—in order to attain the greatest good—God. They're the ones referred to in the Gospel when it says, "The Kingdom of Heaven has suffered violence, and men of violence take it by force." (Mt 11:12)

Let me elaborate on one shining example. Thomas More was a literary scholar, eminent lawyer, high-profile statesman, father of four children and Lord Chancellor of England. A man of unquestioned probity, he would not acknowledge King Henry VIII's divorce from Catherine of Aragon in order to marry the object of his infatuation, Anne Boleyn (recall the 2003 romantic drama film *The Other Boleyn Girl*). When Pope Clement VII refused to annul the king's marriage to Catherine, affirming the indissolubility of the marital bond, Henry VIII broke ties with Rome. An *Act of Succession* (requiring people to recognize the children of

Henry and Anne as legitimate heirs to the throne) was passed in tandem with the *Oath of Supremacy* (binding all English subjects to accept Henry as the Supreme Head of the Church of England). Thomas upheld the dictate of his conscience and refused to take the vow. Prolonged incarceration didn't cow him into bending the truth. Thomas' own wife and several friends tried to persuade him to take the oath and save his life. But he wouldn't budge, undeterred by threats. A kangaroo court found him guilty of treason and condemned him to death by guillotine. Moments before his beheading on July 6, 1535, Thomas declared: "I am the King's good servant, but God's first."[10] To the executioner, he said humorously: "My neck is very short. So be careful not to strike awry…"

Jesus' words of caution to his disicples were fulfilled to the letter in the life of Thomas More: "I send you out as sheep in the midst of wolves; so be wise as serpents and innocent as doves." (Mt 10:16) Saint John Paul II aptly named Thomas as the patron of political leaders in a bid to instill among public authorities the importance of moral rectitude.

Life won't surely test our fortitude in a crucible like Thomas More's. Anyway many people now need not be forced to renounce their faith; they do so as a matter of lifestyle. But we're all called to a different kind of martyrdom—the heroism to fulfill our ordinary tasks and bear the pinpricks of daily life. We might be quick to roll our sleeves up when it comes to helping disaster victims. But how diligent are we to wash the dishes, do our homework, pay the bills and do countless other routine tasks? These are the usual ways to exercise the virtue of fortitude, heroism in the little things, doing what we ought to do here and now.

Courage is much needed in times of war. But one may also need it to declare love. On a Valentine's Day in Paris, one thousand five hundred "In Case of Emergency" boxes containing red roses were fanned out in romantic areas. What for? In case of love at first sight, you could just break the glass and take the flower. Then declare your love with fortitude!

Time to Thole

According to Scholastic philosophers, the immediate subject of the virtue of fortitude is the *irascible appetite*—that which deals with the arduous (hard to attain) good, or good in the face of an evil to be conquered. Its end is to shut out the crippling effect of passion like fear so as to obtain the good grasped by reason. The truly strong person is not the robust and muscular, but one who can face the dreadful. Fortitude involves attack (*aggredi*) and endurance (*sustinere*) as its proper acts, but especially the latter, for it implies the ability to resist the threat and withstand the trials.[11] The apostles of Christ boldly declared they would die with and for Him. But at the moment of truth, they all scampered for safety. Only Mary, other pious women and John, the youngest disciple, stood at the foot of the Cross.

This brings us to the concept of patience (from the Latin *pati*, to suffer), another potential part of the virtue of fortitude. If we can get rid of an evil, let's quash it by all means! But there are times when we're left with no other choice but just support the test.[12] To endure a trial, to bear the pain with little or no complaint, is not to be passive, much less coward. Outwardly we may appear inert, but only because circumstances tie our hands.

Viktor Frankl wrote a book, *Man's Search for Meaning*, that has sold millions of copies. It describes the author's horrible experience in Nazi concentration camps. Starvation, humiliation, fear and anger crushed the hope of most inmates to survive. Everyone was driven to despair, except those who refused to give up what couldn't be snatched away—one's inner freedom and dignity. The fetters can't violate the core of our being if we hold on.[13]

Forbearance is the ability to bear pain calmly. "Afflicted in every way, but not crushed; perplexed, but not driven to despair; persecuted, but not foresaken; struck down, but not destroyed." (2 Cor 4:8-9)

Patience is an important ingredient in daily life. We often lose our inner peace because our plans get waylaid or we want to rush things. We're fidgety and restless. And the usual cause of that long face is attachment to some petty stuff. Let go of it! We gain inner freedom the moment we stop clinging to false idols. Patience is a true source of interior serenity.

Sometimes the best course of action is just to wait. Let things take their natural course. A friend posted the following on her Facebook wall: "I believe that the Lord has ordained certain times and seasons for everything. A baby needs nine months in his mother's womb and being born prematurely brings on complications. You can't pull out an emerging butterfly from its cocoon or else you'll cripple its wings for life. Hurrying a fruit to ripen doesn't make it as sweet as when it does so on its own. Waiting is one of the hardest things to do, but it's the rightest thing to get a perfect blessing."

Stick to the Good

It's a noble thing to bear the contradictions meekly, but we don't suffer for the heck of it. The essence of fortitude is not suffering, but adherence to the moral good,[14] sticking it out all the way to the end. The virtue keeps us intact even if we are beleaguered and hemmed in from all sides. We may be edified by one's habitual tranquility, but there's nothing like the man who keeps his cool in times of distress. Our inmost and deepest strength is shown not when things go smoothly, but when we endure severe tests.[15] The best sailors, they say, do not navigate in calm lakes but rough seas.

In the same vein, fortitude is not a tool to help one in bad pursuits, but in seeking what's good. It's a virtue after all. A student who has the *nerve* to cheat in a proctored exam is no good. Robbers who *dare* swoop into a tightly secured bank are no good. Pregnant women who muster the *courage* to abort their babies are no good. A writer who *painstakingly* collects data to write a slanderous article is no good. They're all barefaced cowards.

Many people do great sacrifices for the wrong thing. So they waste time, energy and money. Endure if we must, but let it be for a real and higher good or a just cause! Fortitude has nothing to do with suffering for vanity's sake. If we want a model of virtue, we won't pick an image-conscious gal given to costly and risky cosmetic procedures just so she would look fabulous. Neither the guy who overstrains himself in a strenuous fitness program in a desperate attempt to become the next poster boy. Fortitude is something else.

The strong man has a big heart that inclines him to undertake bold projects, taxing jobs and great deeds.

He is magnanimous (from *magnus animus*, great soul). But he is not a social climber who boasts of his track record. Neither praise nor criticism affects him much. His only concern is to serve.

Breaking the glass implies violence, the use of force. But the strength of fortitude is not destructive but constructive. It's a violence needed to firm up a soft character, tear down walls of comfort and energize a sluggish attitude. Sometimes we're so lazy that we literally have to drag our feet just to answer a phone call or open the door. We feel the heaviness of our bodies, perhaps overcome by fatigue, such that even the simplest task costs us enormous effort. But it can also be due to indolence. Thus, another potential part of fortitude is laboriosity.

We tend to get excited with anything novel. Going to school for the opening class and meeting new friends. Settling in a different city and greeting new neighbors. Reporting for a new job and sitting at your desk for the first time. Buying new clothes and trying them on. Or watching the first episodes of a new TV series. There is thrill, expectation, kindness, care for details, good motivation and desire to do things well.

But how long does the spark of enthusiasm last? The daily monotony soon takes its toll. We grow weary. The hard toil saps our energy and bit by bit we slow down. We seem to lose interest. Boredom sets in. There's a feeling of uselessness. Our attention and interest shift. We lose our focus. The busy schedule gives room to idle moments. We want something more meaningful. We long for a fresh start. Move elsewhere perhaps. Try something new. And we're back to square one in a recurring cycle in which many people are trapped.

When this happens, we need the spur of laboriosity or diligence. When we like what we do, our performance level shores up. But we don't call it quits when mood swings descend upon us. We have duties to fulfill. A sense of commitment pushes us to overcome lassitude and deliver what's expected of us. It's important to set work targets. The daily routine, the wear and tear, may deplete our energy. That's normal. So we must know, too, how to rest and unwind. But soon we go back to the usual grind with a firm resolve to carry out our habitual tasks. Foster the desire to serve! Rekindle that drive for excellence! That's loyalty. That's perseverance. That's diligence (from the Latin verb *diligo*, to love; hence, to work with love).[16]

If you need an inspiration, you don't have to look far. That colony of ants you see in the corner teaches us valuable lessons on hard work. They have no time cards nor bonus pay nor merit system, but they are amazingly efficient and organized. The Book of Proverbs bids us to consider the ways of these tiny insects if we want to grow in wisdom. (Cf. Prov 6:6)

Fortitude, as we can see, is the virtue that pushes you and me to do what has to be done, to make things happen. Whether it is a question of political "will" to institute reforms, "determination" to graduate, "courage" to speak up, "patience" to wait or "resilience" amidst financial setbacks, what is called for is the strength of fortitude. One way or another, we have to break the glass of comfort, fear, impatience and sloth to brave the storms and weariness of life.

---

[1] *Catechism of the Catholic Church*, no. 1808.

[2] Josef Pieper, *The Four Cardinal Virtues*. Indiana: University of Notre Dame Press, 1966, p. 117.

[3] William J. Bennett (ed.), *The Book of Virtues: A Treasury of Great Moral Stories*. New York: Simon & Schuster, 1993, p. 476.

[4] St. Josemaría Escrivá, *Friends of God*, no. 77.

[5] Donald De Marco, *The Many Faces of Virtue*. Ohio: Emmaus Road Publishing, 2000, p. 42.

[6] A limiting line that when crossed commits a person irrevocably. Rubicon is a river in northern Italy forming part of the border between Gaul and Italy whose crossing by Julius Caesar in 49 B.C. was regarded by the Roman Senate as a declaration of war against Rome. Cf. Bennett (ed.), *op. cit.*, p. 477.

[7] Pieper, *op. cit.*, p. 126.

[8] Celestine Bittle, *Man and Morals*. Milwaukee: The Bruce Publishing Company, 1950, p. 265.

[9] Second Vatican Council, *Gaudium et spes* (1965), no. 17.

[10] http://www.americancatholic.org/Features/Saints/saint.aspx?id=1422 and http://catholiceducation.org/articles/religion/re0559.html and http://www.catholicnewsagency.com/saint.php?n=499.

[11] St. Thomas Aquinas, *Summa Theologiae*, IIa-IIae, q. 61, a. 1-3; q. 123, a. 3-6.

[12] Pieper, *op. cit.*, pp. 128-129.

[13] Victor Frankl, *Man's Search for Meaning*. New York: Pocket Books, 1963, pp. 106-107.

[14] St. Thomas Aquinas, *Summa Theologiae*, IIa-IIae, q. 123, a. 1.

[15] Pieper, *op. cit.*, p. 130.

[16] Manuel Belda, *Guiados por el espíritu de Dios*. Madrid: Ediciones Palabra, S.A., 2006, p. 258.

Chapter Six

DRINK MODERATELY

I was in the third grade of primary school when I first encountered the word "moderately" in an English class. That day our teacher (of happy memory) taught us a lesson on adverbs. So the next time I saw the word, in a TV commercial, I literally sprang up on my feet to trumpet to everyone in the living room: "I know that word!" I waited to hear compliments for my "advanced" vocabulary, but there was none. Only my older brother butted in nonchalantly: "I learned that in second grade."

The TV ad promoted Johnnie Walker Scotch Whisky as an excellent liquor brand, but with a stern postscript—"Drink Moderately!" I turned to my dad with an inquisitive mind: "Dad, why limit the sales of their product? I don't get it." His reply was clever but evasive: "They don't tell us to buy less, only to drink less." Dad liked Johnnie Walker.

Years later I learned that bottles of liquor bear health warning labels in compliance with a government mandate. But it was only in Moral Theology class, particularly on the cardinal moral virtue of temperance, that I finally grasped the full import of Johnnie Walker's little caveat: "Drink Moderately."

From Use to Abuse

We all take this warning sign as plain public service. But it has rich philosophical-anthropological content. The label "Drink Moderately" prods us to take it easy. Enjoy, but be sober! Have fun, but don't go overboard! Implied in this notice is the reality that we're all prone to excesses. Oh yes, we do have a penchant to overindulge, be it in beverages or food delights or anything else we like. It's our inherent human weakness, abetted by a fallen nature that breeds all kinds of disorder. The adhesive stamp may very well be reworded as "eat moderately" and attached to every plate in a buffet restaurant. Or "watch moderately" and plastered on a cable TV. Or "drive moderately" and glued to the dashboard of vehicles. The Pope even hinted at "surf moderately" to computer geeks addicted to web surfing. We can attach this sticker to laptops and desktops.

You and I have natural powers, desires and urges. On the one hand we have animal appetites like our craving for victuals. We share this inclination with the canine, feline and equine. Because we are material, sensitive beings, we seek what gratifies our bodily senses. Hence, we like to see (watch a TV show, look at the skyscrapers, stare at a pretty lady, ogle at jewels), touch (feel the texture, hold the gadget, lay our hand on a motorbike, caress the baby), smell (sniff the flowers, scent the perfume), hear (listen to music, eavesdrop on a conversation), and taste (savor beef curry or vanilla ice cream).

But on the other hand, we are endowed with a rational intellect and a free will. Unlike the beasts, we think and reflect. Dignity. Feelings. Emotions. Love. Sacrifice. Only humans possess or are capable of these.

We seek to know things (Google search, ask for directions, study a subject, draw inferences) and make choices (pick a shoe brand, decide on a career, select whom to marry). Civilized as we are, we have a sense of honor and a sense of shame. We try to keep the ABC's of good manners and right conduct that we all learned in kindergarten.

All these qualities make us distinctively human, called to a higher form of life than sheer animal existence. You might be fond of kittens and puppies, but don't forget that you're a rational creature, a reasoning being. And you're expected to behave as such. It's our task to regulate our base instincts so that the spiritual prevails over the animal. In the composite of body and soul that we're all made of, the latter is the nobler part tasked to govern our raw, brute tendencies.[1]

This is easier said than done. Often the sense experience is so overpowering as to eclipse the soul. We seek whatever we find attractive, gratifying and pleasurable, and relish it to the max, even beyond what's healthy and reasonable. We're not theorizing here. Our own experiences attest to this reality. We have all had our fair share of immoderation. Perhaps you're often glued to your favorite TV series till the wee hours of the morning, never mind being groggy the next day. Or you're so hooked to computer games as to set aside urgent school work. Or impulse drives you to fill the shopping cart with items on sale, only to realize back home that you don't really need them. Or you have the habit of surreptitiously devouring a sandwich or chocolate bar at odd hours of the day even though your stomach is full.

It's perfectly alright to go shopping, watch movies, puff cigarettes, savor choice dishes and sip ardent spirits if we set proper limits. What's wrong is not their use, but their abuse. We're wont to discipline the kids, telling them "that's enough!" when they give in to infantile whims. Yet we ourselves lack self-moderation. When we overindulge, what's normal becomes abnormal, the good turns vicious and our behavior is marked by extremes. Whatever prompts us to go a little wild in self-satisfying activities, it's definitely not healthy. Vices grow. Spiritual blindness obscures our mind. We become insensitive to others. Sloth gets the better of us. We lack focus. Sensuality is aroused. The world begins to revolve around "me, myself, mine" in a stifling cycle of egoism. Our capacity to do good tapers off. Plus we turn irritable, selfish, dishonest and irreverent. Immoderation is losing hold of oneself. It is a perfect recipe for self-destruction.

Don't throw the blame on marketing propaganda or peer pressure! Like attack dogs kept on chains, all they can do is bark; they can't bite us if we keep to a safe distance. The key is self-possession. Learn the art of self-control! It's actually possible to mingle with the world without falling prey to its venomous tentacles. The problem is that we are so weak. Unaccustomed to a virtuous life, we're easily swept away by hedonistic currents. So instead of being free, we end up slaves, held captive by our low passions, dominated by the animal part within.

Benjamin Franklin put "temperance" on top of his list of 13 virtues when he crafted a self-improvement program. How come? He believed that to gain self-discipline, one must start with his or her most basic appetite and work up from there. We need to first harness our inner impulses before dealing with the more outward things.[2]

Magnet of Pleasure

We yield to our desires because of the thrill and satisfaction we get. Pleasure is like a powerful magnet. It pulls us and keeps us hooked to anything we find fascinating. Intense pleasure can have a blinding effect for the weak-willed and malformed. Pleasure is quite normal, even necessary and desirable to some extent. We need not be surprised that a lot of our natural activities are gratifying. God arranged things that way—for a reason.

Temperance has bad publicity for it is often held out as a repression of natural human inclinations, like the Stoics of old for whom all pleasures were evil. No. To be temperate is to domesticate, not kill or cage the wild, unruly beast within us. We try to tame it so that it serves rather than threatens us. To use another analogy, we can't stop the cascading waters of a rough river, but we can channel its flow, direct its course and so use it to our advantage.

Sense pleasure is most powerful in two areas: food and sex. The palate (needed for self-preservation) and the genitalia (needed for the propagation of the human species) give rise to two dominant passions, two primal urges at work in every man and woman. A person might enjoy doing an adrenalin-pumping dare-devil sport; or be so passionate about owning a limited edition collectors' item; or eager for the next leisure trip to Hawaii, Maldives or the Bahamas. But no human drive is as potent as eating and the sexual act, no other experience more intense than what corresponds to these two important organic functions.

Imagine if the simple act of eating or drinking were unpleasant instead of delectable; we would soon be skin and bones, thin as a rail. We would have to be coaxed to eat. So too, the sexual act comes with pleasure that serves as a stimulus for men and women to willingly become parents and form a family. Otherwise, society will have to come up with all sorts of creative incentives just so couples would match. If the use of the sexual faculty were boring rather than enjoyable, very few, if any, would beget children, planet earth would be depopulated and the human race would eventually fizzle out.[3] God knew better.

So pleasure is not bad per se. It surely has a good use and noble function. But here's the catch. We're in deep trouble when we seek pleasure for its own sake, when it ceases to be the means to an end and becomes an end in itself. This is moral suicide. Making pleasure the primary goal in life is a trash proposition of the hedonistic culture so pervasive in today's world. The unbridled quest for comfort and pleasure spells the ruin of many lives. For love of pleasure, men and women go crazy, blind and wayward. Horrible crimes and shameful infidelities are the upshot of runaway, almost pathological quest for pleasure.

One of the greatest ironies in human life is the fact that our powers of self-preservation—eating to keep oneself alive, and sex to keep the human species alive—can be the very same sources of self-destruction. Because these forces are closely allied to the deepest human urge toward being, they are unsurpassed in destructive potential when they go awry—when the proper, upright, selfless self-preservation intrinsic to eating and sex degenerates into unbridled, pervert and selfish forms of self-assertion.[4] Gluttony and unchastity are first cousins. A person who can't control his food appetite also generally falls into sexual indiscretion, just as the one who is able to mortify himself over the table can more readily ward off carnal charms.

Let us learn from history. The apogee of the Roman Empire had a major drawback: its moral decadence. Basking in their glorious military conquests, the Romans grew complacent. Corrupt customs were the order of the day. Lifestyle spiraled downwards. Promiscuity and gluttony were aplenty. Grand banquets were organized where people could eat *ad nauseam*. Seneca denounced the disgusting practice of those who "vomit that they may eat, and eat that they may vomit." Emperor Vitellius, whose reign was short-lived circa 69 A.D., was touted as the Imperial Glutton for giving lavish feasts in the imperial palace. He ate four heavy meals a day. He taught people how to live in order to eat. He dispatched naval expeditions just to procure rare foods he craved for. One of his favorite dishes was the "Shield of Minerva"—a salad-supreme made of the "liver of charfish, the brains of pheasants and peacocks, the tongues of flamingoes, and the entrails of lampreys." Good thing he did not last long, or else the imperial coffers would have gone bankrupt with his extravagance.[5]

The Roman hoggish regales missed the natural purpose of eating, which is nourishment, not pleasure. To throw up what one eats in order to swallow more is to separate the biological process of digestion from the eating function. To modern ears the Roman revelry is degrading, repugnant. Nowadays we see none of this. But our society has its own subtle ways to spur us on to gluttony. Satisfy your cravings! Eat all you can! Bottomless drink! Unlimited rice! These are typical come-ons of diners, grills and cafés around the city. And of course, the *Guinness Book of World Records* decorates the man who can devour the most number of hotdogs in a time-trial eating contest.

I find it a little odd that many people spend hours in the fitness gym doing strenuous workouts just to reduce their waistlines and flatten their tummies, yet easily offset their weight loss by the uncontrolled intake of oily and high-calorie foods. Here are practical tips from a book entitled *The Art of Manliness*: "Eat when hungry, stop when full. Don't eat in front of the TV or on the go. Sit down for a proper meal. Savor each mouthful, and think about the flavors you are experiencing. Put your fork down between bites. When…your stomach starts to feel full, stop eating." When it comes to beverages, the book suggests that we "drink not to elevation." Real men don't have any dependencies, especially alcoholism. They don't need liquid courage to create fun, have a good time, appear charming or gain confidence.[6]

How about sex for pleasure? Well, the same principle holds. The sexual faculty is naturally ordained to a communion of love and the transmission of life. To delink sex from its inherent purpose is a grave disorder.[7] Sadly, lifestyles are too common that hanker for venereal pleasure for its own sake, which is sex without love—casual sex, flings, friends with benefits, and sex without kids—thanks to pills and condoms.

A young fellow had just come back from a holiday in Las Vegas, where sex, drink and gambling are celebrated. The city is loud and hot; it stinks. Chatting with his former mentor, the adolescent confided that he grappled with temptations while living in the sin city. His adviser said: "You'll be fine as long as you don't entertain them." "Oh, I don't entertain them," he retorted with a tinge of irony, "they entertain me."

Sometimes things are not as brazen. Subtle innuendoes are used to lure, like the spa and massage parlor a few blocks from my office. It has a signboard at the entrance: "Come and indulge in an experience that will pamper you senses!" Macho culture also fosters vanity and sensuality that trump a person's spiritual life. It's okay to try to stay fit and look good, but quite another thing to get so engrossed in wellness and fitness, spending lavishly on assorted skin and facial products, cosmetic and liposuction centers, in the quest for flawless, wrinkle-free baby skin, enduring a rigorous gym regimen in a desperate attempt to halt one's aging, maintain six-pack abs or a slim, beach body figure—as if physical prowess and beauty were all that mattered in life. Beware of the neo-pagan cult and idolatry of the human body for which everything else is sacrificed.[8]

Sexual temperance or chastity is the antidote to sexual immoderation. Chastity is not meant to weaken the power of sexual faculty but to harness it for a good end. This virtue has nothing to do with a dull personality and boring life. Romantic attraction may be strong and yet pure. Largely forgotten, chastity unwraps the hidden beauty of human sexuality. God made us either *male* or *female* in a mutual complementarity of biological, psychological and emotional constitutions. We share the same humanity, but differ in sexual identity. Man and woman join to become "one flesh" through a reciprocal donation of oneself in the context of conjugal love, a life-long alliance that is open to life. When true love reigns, there's no room for self-serving behavior that treats one's partner as a mere object of pleasure.

Slogans like "True Love Waits" or "Romance Without Regrets" are a call to chastity. And it's consoling to know that countless men and women, boys and girls all over the world are rallying behind a new sexual revolution—the crusade for sexual purity. So much for debauchery clad in freedom!

Corollary to chastity is modesty, the virtue that regulates our external deportment, inclining us to observe what's proper in conduct, movement, speech, posture, dress and entertainment.[9] It's the virtue that keeps us discreet and reasonably reserved. We do well when we hide what must not be exposed. Respect your own privacy! I wonder why people have to tweet every move they make or post on Facebook stuff they do in the kitchen or bathroom. The "selfie" generation has lots of insecurities, it seems. They always seek approval and acceptance. Just click "like" and that makes their day.

Can you tell what's common among the following? A loudmouth laughing boisterously in a meeting; a gate-crasher voraciously eating a plateful in a party; and a boozy woman in a flirtatious mood hanging out at a late hour. We feel ashamed for them, right? They all need to be modest. In fashion, the battle for modesty is uphill, what with the generalized moral laxity where the skimpy, vulgar, casual and popular are the dominant ethos.

Pope Francis made the world smile with his disarming candor and out-of-the-box approach to the wayward and the frail. But he pulled no punches when he pointed out errors: "In the prevailing culture," the Holy Father wrote in *Evangelii Gaudium*, "priority is given to the outward, the immediate, the visible, the quick, the superficial and the provisional. What is real gives way to appearances... Globalization has meant a hastened deterioration of...cultural roots and the invasion of ways of thinking and acting that are ethically debilitated."[10]

Healthy Balance

Often the word "temperance" is equated with "restraint" and "self-control." This idea can be misleading. When a girl is anorexic and emaciated for not eating well, she needs temperance (and perhaps medication) to remedy her food deficiency, for neglect of one's bodily health is not a virtue. But so does the lazy, fat gobbler whose only joy in life seems to be swallowing mouthfuls in smorgasbords. This one, too, is intemperate—but by excess. Temperance fixes our inner disorder and puts balance among our scattered senses, passions and faculties. It smoothens, as it were, the wrinkles and protrusions, cavities and bulges of our behavior and allows us to enjoy the good things in life in their right measure. We study enough, play enough, work enough, rest enough and eat enough.[11] The key is balance. Equilibrium. Proper amount. Neither lavish nor inadequate.

If temperance usually connotes self-control, it's because we lack self-restraint just as often. The naughty little child inside us, the immature "me" throws tantrums every so often. Intractable. Vain. Whimsical. Capricious. Euphemism conveniently calls our excesses unguarded moments, natural impulses, knee-jerk reactions, unconscious habits. But the bare bones of all these is a lack of self-dominion. Somehow we have remained a child all these years, mature in age perhaps but retarded and infantile in character. No wonder we uncritically go with the fad, "tossed to and fro and carried about by every wind of doctrine." (Eph 4:14)

Like any other virtue, the goal of temperance is to help us live an upright life. One is not being temperate by stealing less money, abating lies and reducing pornography. In a sense, yes, the less evil we commit, the better. But temperance is sobriety in licit things, not retaining a mitigated form of vice.

Some people do not have serious bouts with gluttony and lust. They have good eating habits. Temptations of the flesh aren't much of an issue. Buy they're hot-tempered. Irascible. Choleric. Trigger-happy. They blow their top at the slightest provocation, real or perceived. They get extremely annoyed if something or someone gets in their way, if they are contradicted, if their plans are thwarted. That irritation lasts for as long as the obstacle is there. They then use everything in their power to get rid of it. Anger drives them to regain their territory and secure their interest.

As a passion, anger is not essentially evil. Anger is good if it's reasonable and serves the true good of man. It's certainly better to be fiery about something good than to be passive and indifferent about it.[12] We naturally get mad when, for example, we see a big man beating up a little child, or if an old beggar in a street corner is ridiculed by some rowdy youth, or if we catch someone trying to swindle us. Our Lord Jesus himself was angry more than once.

But anger turns ugly when it becomes blind wrath. That's when ire breaks all bounds and disrupts the order of reason. Often this goes with bitterness of spirit and vengeful resentment. Facts are ignored, judgment is clouded, there's a violent upsurge of self-will, and the heart is poisoned like a festering ulcer.[13]

When this happens, temperance comes to the rescue, armed with gentleness and meekness to master the power of wrath and overcome vindictiveness.[14] To be gentle is not to look harmless and pale-faced, much less to be soft in character. Meekness teaches us to be mild mannered and be angry—when we have to—in the proper way.

Temperance also curbs our tendency to self-exaltation—to pride—on the strength of humility. Egoism is a disordered self-love that inclines us to magnify our qualities and claim credits beyond what we truly deserve. The fact is, no matter how brilliant we are or how many trophies we have, so many other people can boast of a better track record. We look great only relative to the shortcomings of others. "No man rises on the strength of his bootstraps alone. Innate talent and lucky breaks, coupled with a supportive family, friend, teacher or coach, always contribute somewhere down the line… A humble man doesn't always have to be the biggest toad in the puddle. He understands that others have equally interesting stories to share, and his turn will come."[15]

Humility is an inner disposition that acknowledges one's capacity and limitations. Humble individuals know how to say "thank you." They shun being in the spotlight. They don't show off their talents or mask their defects. Neither do they hide what must be laid out, including their God-given talents. A potential part of temperance, humility gives us an estimation of ourselves according to the truth, nothing more, nothing less.

Temperance covers still a wider scope. Nietzche once said that wisdom puts limits to knowledge. We don't really know what he meant by that. But our desire to know, that most noble faculty of human intellect, needs to be checked too. This is not to lament learning and education. The *locus* of this unrestrained quest to know lies in the concupiscence of the eyes. We are gifted with vision so we can perceive reality. Obviously the sense of sight is in itself good. But disorder is introduced by concupiscence when we seek the pleasure of seeing, when we watch, stare, look and ogle simply because we enjoy doing so. Curiosity is its name. It is seeing not in order to attain knowledge, but to wallow in the world.[16]

A former office colleague was dubbed as "walking encyclopedia" because he knew heaps about the American War of Independence, the ancient Etruscan people, plate tectonics, oil paintings, butterfly farms, poetry, Rolex and Omega watches, Formula 1 and many more. Of course he had spent much of his youth reading books and magazines and he had a photographic memory. But there was a downside. His addiction to reading meant sleepless nights, tardiness in the office, delayed reports, an air of pedantry and disdain towards those who knew less. Worse, he dug deep into things he shouldn't have, stuff that spoiled his soul. The quest for knowledge is co-natural to us, intellectual beings. It's a virtue to be studious. But temperance has to step in whenever *studiositas* degenerates into *curiositas*.

Our competitive society pushes us to be up-to-date, catch the latest news and trends, and be aware of the in-thing. So we frequently surf the Internet, open the broadsheets and read magazines to be informed. But it's not about absorbing a plethora of data. It's wise to choose what to read and process the information. For one, it's physically impossible to read everything. For another, a lot of things written are trash. Temperance regulates one's hunger to know and helps one focus on the more essential and useful stuff.

We have seen so far that temperance restrains our proclivity to excesses in self-preservation: inordinate desire for or too much food, sex, anger, self-love and knowledge. There's one more area where temperance is much needed—the use of earthly goods.

When I was in senior high school, I remember a top-billed song played over and over by FM radio stations and hummed by young people all over—Madonna's *Material Girl* (1984, Sire Records), the song that, together with *Like A Virgin*, made her a popular icon. The lyrics expressed her quest for a rich and affluent life. By sheer osmosis, I myself chanted *a material girl in a material world* while walking down the campus corridors. Back then I had no idea what values the song was spreading. Now I know. Madonna encapsulates in her song the spirit of materialism and consumerism that has gripped modern society.

People generally enjoy material possessions. In a sense, it's part of our natural vocation to exercise dominion over the earth. We try to earn and procure things in order to survive, live in a dignified way and secure our future. Ownership of private property is a basic human right. We are also attracted to material things because of their natural beauty. Everything we find on Mother Earth bears the goodness of its Creator. That much Philosophy teaches us.

But then again we tend to overstep the bounds. Our hearts get attached to things when we forget their instrumental nature (i.e., means to an end) and seek them as ends in themselves. When we set our heart on something, we're restless until we possess it. That intense pining becomes a form of idolatry especially when it takes our attention off the more important things like family and religious duties. The object of obsession can be a cutting edge smartphone, a signature handbag, the top of the line SUV or an upscale villa. One can also go crazy over a fashionable shoe brand, an exquisite perfume or a popular reality show. Not only those with deep pockets though, are prone to greed. The have-nots can also cling inordinately to a paltry possession and be gripped by the specter of materialism. Covetousness is a common human frailty.

Of course the heart can also yearn for money, fame, distinction, title, position and success. Everything and anything that bolsters one's ego and personal security. Like a true miser, we can even hoard a pen, bracelet, photo, mirror, pin, sweater, pendant and trinkets of all kinds. Those trifles stored in your closet all this time: what are they for?

The virtue of temperance moderates our desire for earthly goods and worldly satisfactions through detachment and a spirit of poverty.[17] We aren't asked to despise created things.[18] The world and everything natural in it is wonderful. But human dignity requires that we attain self-mastery, part of which is dominion over things, not slavery to them. "This way of seeing things is a safeguard against the spirit of luxury, the love of goods for themselves, which often brings with it envy of those who have more and ostentation in showing off one's own goods."[19]

We are truly *poor in spirit* if we consider ourselves as steward, rather than the absolute owner, of our possessions. The best antidote to greed and avarice is a spirit of detachment as shown in living a simple and sober life, as well as being generous with others, especially the needy. It pays to practice voluntary austerity. The Holy Writ exhorts us to reject worldly lusts and live in a way sober, upright and Godly in this world. (Cf. Tit 2:12)

Wise Label

Many of our past errors stemmed from a lack of self-control. The hurtful words we blurted out, those episodes of impulsive buying, our quick temper that strained friendly relations, the thoughtless actions, arrogant bearings, unhealthy curiosities, malicious touches, immodest outfits, bad promises, hasty decisions and indiscreet remarks.

Temperance invites us to look deep into our inner self and set things right. It's a lifetime task to align our passions with right reason (enlightened by faith), putting them back on track each time they go berserk owing to our wounded nature. This is the most profound meaning of the Latin word *temperantia* and its closest Greek equivalent *sophrosyne* which means "directing reason." The virtue strikes a proper balance among the different parts of the whole man, body and soul, and bridles the tendency of the lower appetites to go wild.[20] Integral unity and inner harmony is achieved, making it possible for the human person to reach one's final end. We may feel the pinch caused by temperance, especially if it means giving up something so dear to us. But it's worth the sacrifice. This virtue is a *conditio sine qua non* for us to achieve our full human potential. There's real spiritual growth only if we strive to be the master of our passions, not their vassals.[21]

It pays to foster a healthy form of "self-distrust." We don't mean trampling on self-esteem. Often what we like to do is not what we should really do. Stick to duty when preference demands its way! Love of comfort entices us to delay our tasks, make short cuts, minimize our work, prolong our rest, grab the best share and avoid accountability. Yet we rave about having a good time. We thus need a good mix of fortitude and temperance. A firm character develops when we get to say "no" to our whims and caprice. When others want instant gratification, it's wise to be patient. You'll surely smile the moment you learn how to make do with what you have and appreciate the joy of simple living.

Life then takes on again shades and tones which intemperance had tended to blur...Temperance makes the soul sober, modest, understanding. It fosters a natural sense of reserve which everyone finds attractive because it denotes an intelligent self-control.[22]

A person who has achieved self-mastery is serene and he radiates that peace to others. He is emotionally stable, well able to control his reactions, modulate the tone of his voice, rise above petty squabbles, settle for less comfort and wait for one's turn. Temperance allows us to say the right word at the right time in the right way. Decisions are well pondered. We're not carried away by sentimental roller-coaster. We think straight and hold fast to our principles. We shun fanciful and extravagant lifestyles. We don't do things we would soon regret. Patience keeps us calm when expectations are unmet. It's not our stuff to hanker for wealth and fame, but thank heaven if they come anyway. People in need can turn to us for help. We're happy to share what we have. We may be fond of certain things but we don't suffer if we're not meant to have them, thanks to an inner freedom that gives us a rare capacity for detachment. Those around us may stare at anything flashy and fabulous, but we can look elsewhere without feeling deprived. We're content with ordinary things. We look with a pure gaze and love with a pure heart. Most of all, a temperate soul is attuned to the voice of God, disposed to pray and live a holy life.

There's truly a lot of hidden wisdom in Johnnie Walker Scotch Whisky's monitory label: "Drink Moderately."

---

[1] Celestine Bittle, *Man and Morals*. Milwaukee: The Bruce Publishing Company, 1950, p. 262.

[2] Brett McKay and Kate McKay, *The Art of Manliness: Classic Skills and Manners for the Modern Man*. Ohio: HOW Books, 2009, p. 235.

[3] Bittle, *op. cit.*, pp. 262-263.

[4] Josef Pieper, *The Four Cardinal Virtues*. Indiana: University of Notre Dame Press, 1966, p. 150.

[5] William Stearns Davis, *A Day in Old Rome: A Picture of Roman Life*. New York: Biblo & Tannen Publishers, 1959, p. 102.

[6] McKay and McKay, *op. cit.*, pp. 235-236.

[7] Juan Luis Lorda, *Moral: El Arte de Vivir*. Madrid: Ediciones Palabra, S.A., 2006, pp. 162-163.

[8] *Catechism of the Catholic Church*, no. 2289.

[9] Bittle, *op. cit.*, p. 264.

[10] Pope Francis, Apostolic Exhortation *Evangelii Gudium* (2013), no. 64.

[11] Linda Kavelin Popov, *The Family Virtues Guide*. New York: Penguin Group, 1997, p. 185.

[12] Pieper, *op. cit.*, p. 194.

[13] *Ibid.*, p. 195.

[14] Bittle, *op. cit.*, p. 264.

[15] McKay and McKay, *op. cit.*, pp. 262-263.

[16] Pieper, *op. cit.*, p. 200.

[17] Manuel Belda, *Guiados por el espíritu de Dios*. Madrid: Ediciones Palabra, S.A., 2006, pp. 84-85.

[18] *Ibid.*, p. 84.

[19] Juan Luis Lorda, *The Virtues of Holiness: The Basics of Spiritual Struggle*. New York: Scepter Publishers, 2010, p. 24.

[20] Pieper, *op. cit.*, p. 146.

[21] Leo J. Trese, *Human But Holy: Getting To Know God, Yourself and Your Neighbor*. Manila: Sinag-Tala Publishers, Inc., 1999, p. 37.

[22] St. Josemaría Escrivá, *Friends of God*, no. 84.

CHAPTER SEVEN

IS IT THE TRUTH?

This is the first question of the Four-Way Test we see in strategic locations (city squares, street junctions or town plazas) around the world. The four-pronged code of ethics became part of the emblem of Rotary Club International when Herbert Taylor, author of the code, ceded property rights over it to Rotary International while serving as the organization's president in 1954-55.

Herb was a deeply religious man gifted with excellent leadership and business skills. In 1932, he was asked to help revive a floundering, near-bankrupt Club Aluminum Company in Chicago. He took up the gauntlet with one clear goal in mind: corporate culture must change. So he devised a moral yardstick that could guide personal and business life: the Four-Way Test. Simple in content yet profound in meaning, the principles became the basis for decision making in all levels of the company. Employees learned the Test by heart. It was displayed on desktops. The formula became a corporate byword and served as an inspiration that boosted the morale of a beleaguered company.[1]

Not everybody, though, believed in it. There were debates over its practical value. Wasn't the Four-Way

Test too idealistic in the rough and tumble world of business? Could people be expected to abide by its precepts when money was involved? How could honesty be made a policy where dog-eat-dog was the rule of the game? One lawyer told Herb: "If I followed the Test explicitly, I would starve to death. Where business is concerned, I think the Four-Way Test is absolutely impractical."[2]

But the cookware manufacturing proved him wrong. The Four-Way Test was no utopia. The company staff applied it first to advertising. Words like "better," "best," "greatest" or "finest" were dropped from ads and replaced by objective, more accurate descriptions of the product. Negative remarks about competitors were removed from company literature. Every transaction was gauged by the new standard of ethics. It didn't take long for the Test to create a climate of trust, goodwill and integrity among dealers, customers and employees. Club Aluminum's reputation and finances bounced back to a healthy trend. The firm eventually paid off its huge debt and over the next 15 years distributed over one million dollars in dividends to its stockholders. By 1937 its net worth climbed to more than $2 million.

Since then the Four-way Test has been adopted, translated, reprinted and posted worldwide in schools, companies, clubs and associations. Its call for moral excellence and appeal to integrity are as powerful as ever. Perhaps this is because the Test is a cry from the heart that transcends cultural barriers and political ideologies. It certainly strikes deep at the core of human values. At the 1977 R.I. Convention, James S. Fish of the U.S. Better Business Bureaus said, "To endure, the competitive enterprise system must be practiced within the framework of a strict moral code. Indeed, the whole fabric of the capitalistic system rests to a large degree on trust...on the confidence that businessmen and women will deal fairly and honestly, not only with each other, but also with the general public, with the consumer, the stockholder and the employee."[3]

Calling a Spade, a Spade

Ever since classical Greek philosophy argued that "reason" is the distinguishing mark of the human person, setting him above all other creatures as a "rational animal," world history has been a continuous quest to know the reality of things—the truth about the world, man and God. Endowed with intellect and will, we tend to probe everything under the sun. And we don't stop till we're satisfied.

The human mind is made for the Truth. Universities owe their origin to man's pursuit of knowledge, higher learning and the truth. Court trials, forensic investigations and DNA tests are conducted to ferret out the truth. Research laboratories run experiments and analyze data to discover the truth. The mass media (television, broadcast and print) operate to disseminate the truth. Archeologists dig the earth and examine fossils and artifacts to find out the truth.

There are different kinds or levels of truth. Here I shall focus on the moral truth. It's the conformity of our mind to our words, or the coherence between what we say and what we really think. An honest person is frank and straightforward. His words have no toppings; he calls a spade a spade. Honesty isn't just telling the truth once, twice or occasionally. It means habitual truthfulness. Like any other moral virtue, sincerity is a stable disposition to think, speak and act with candor and genuineness.

Thus, honesty is more than just unsullied speech. The way a person behaves is the litmus test of one's sincerity. This facet of moral life includes a whole range of positive attributes like integrity, loyalty, trustworthiness, fairness, probity and nobility. An honest man doesn't cheat, trick or defraud others, but always acts *bona fide*. We expect him to return the wallet he finds, pay the bus ticket, cite bibliographical sources or keep his appointments. I won't be surprised if he owns the restaurant called Sincerity Café that boasts of genuine Oyster Cake, Shark's Fin Soup and Fresh Salad.

When Herb scribbled the first question of the Four-Way Test, he invited everybody to practice self-examination. The bottom line is, in everything you do, "Are you being honest? Are you true to yourself and your fellowmen?" We may not have to explain ourselves to anyone, but our natural conscience acts like a sentinel watching our every move from within. And it gnaws at us the moment we behave badly. We better check our motives and think twice before doing something we will regret later on.

The question, *Is it the truth?* is followed by three others: 1) *Is it fair to all concerned?* 2) *Will it build goodwill and better friendships?* 3) *Will it be beneficial to all concerned?* The sequence is not random. It follows a real and logical order. The truth of things is prior to considerations of justice or friendship. Healthy relationships are built on mutual trust, which in turn, rests on honesty. Whether you're dealing with a family member, schoolmate, business partner, a neighbor or your own spouse, sincerity is all-important. Without this virtue human relations break down. Dishonesty sows distrust, suspicion and skepticism. This is not rocket science; it's plain common sense. Try lying to a close friend and you risk losing his or her confidence when you're discovered. You may be sorry. He or she may try to let it pass. But often things will hardly be the same as before, all because you lied and he or she got hurt. How could you afford to do that?

You declare your income, profits and losses for the computation of your annual income tax. Is it the truth? You tell the doctor that your chest X-rays have never shown abnormal results in the past. Is it the truth? You apply for a sick leave from the office due "to acute migraine and vertigo attacks." Is it the truth? You phone your wife saying you'll be home late due to a dinner meeting with business clients. Is it the truth? You brag of multiple awards back in high school as the captain of the Debate Team, head of the Physics Society and commander of the Cadet Corps. Is it the truth? Let's make it a point "never to open our mouths except to say what we honestly believe to be true."[4]

Thin Edge of the Wedge

The human person is a social being. We're tailor-made, so to speak, to interact with others. It's difficult, nay, impossible to live alone. Though we take it for granted, we're always communicating with other people. Some are tight-lipped and the introvert type. Others are chatty and hail-fellow-well-met by temperament. But everyone communicates with everybody by talking, calling on the phone, sending SMS or email, chatting on-line, by gestures and body language.

We use the "word" (oral or written) to express our feelings, convey our ideas and pass on information. We assume that what we hear and read is true. We generally consider people as honest and so take their words at face value. If your colleague says, "I'll meet you at Starbucks at 7 p.m.," you believe him without much ado. He may show up a bit late due to traffic or some errands, but to begin with, it's assumed he's not fooling you. So, too, when the concierge at the department store lobby points to you the nearest boutique, you simply follow the directions. And if the teacher announces, "We'll have a short quiz tomorrow," you better be ready. Engaged couples don't feign their feelings when he or she declares, "I love you so much." That's the case *generally*, I said, because the world is full of deceptions, as we shall see.

The *word*, hence, is a vehicle to transmit the moral truth. Living or working together is pleasant when you know that the fellow seated beside you is true to you in all your mutual dealings. Community life in its various forms—academic, family, corporate, conjugal or civic—thrives on honesty and integrity. We realize that the persons we admire most are those who "ring true." Their deportment has no traces of any sham; they act as they really are.[5] The quality that most people seek in a leader is not a handsome face, financial liquidity or academic laurels. It's character integrity.

Lying distorts the truth. It divests the "word" of its inherent function as the standard medium of human communication. Lies deceive people and deprive them of their right to know the truth. Of course, we don't broadcast intimate things nor divulge secrets—matters we're morally bound to keep from people who don't have the right to know them, especially the busybodies and malicious gossips. It's another matter though with perverts and assailants; we better mislead them. Doctors, lawyers, professors and soldiers must keep mum on confidential information they know. But save for these exceptions, we all ought to be plainspoken. Truthfulness is a moral duty. "Let what you say be simply 'Yes' or 'No'; anything more than this comes from the devil." (Mt 5:37)

When our words or actions are at variance with what's on our mind (*locutio contra mentem*), we are trying to perform a trick. By bending the truth, we sow seeds of discord. It's just a matter of time before somebody smells trouble. Relations turn sour. Confidence is lost. Unity is ruptured. When mutual trust is upset, it's not easy, if at all, to restore harmony. A lie may not cause total estrangement at first, but it's often the thin edge of the wedge.

"A lie does real violence to another. It affects his ability to know, which is a condition of every judgment and decision. It contains the seed of discord and all the consequent evils. Lying is destructive of society; it undermines trust among men and tears apart the fabric of social relationships."[6] Which is why veracity is so important in social life. It is an act of interpersonal justice. "The Lord abhors…deceitful men." (Ps 5:6)

I'm a canon lawyer and one ground for declaring a marriage null and void is *simulation*.[7] This happens when one or both spouses tie the knot in wedding rites but don't really have the intention to marry. Marriage by convenience, done for example to allow an alien to enter the United States of America, is a farce. Simulation is a grave form of lying. Imagine if you attend the nuptials as a godparent!

But a lie harms its author more than anyone else. It's a form of self-betrayal in thought and word. One's mind ought to reflect the truth he or she possesses. The words we speak must be the mirror of our own integrity or wholeness. "All dishonesty injures the trustworthiness of the person" and it "goes against the dignity of man."[8] Our personal honor is tarnished when we're not truthful. Besides, when we tell lies, we blow the lid off our inner weakness. We're scared to assume the responsibility of telling the truth.[9] Dishonesty is a lack of fortitude.

Some folks are adept at resorting to smokescreens and subterfuge when they talk or write. It's a linguistic veneer to hide their true selves, their real motives. Others fabricate false information by force of habit. Or they intentionally leave out some crucial data. False fronts. Double talk. Cover-ups. "You speak a half-truth which is open to so many interpretations that it can really be called…a lie."[10] Jesus emphatically warns us against all forms of insincerity and duplicity: "Woe to you, scribes and Pharisees, hypocrites! For you are like whitewashed tombs, which outwardly appear beautiful, but within, they are full of dead men's bones and all uncleanness. So you also outwardly appear righteous to men, but within you are full of hypocrisy and iniquity." (Mt 23:27-28) On the other hand, Our Lord praised those who are simple and honest, like Nathanael, "an Israelite indeed, in whom is no guile!" (Jn 1:47)

Sine Cera

If it's already bad enough to tell officious lies (lies told to obtain an advantage), it's a lot worse to make false statements that stain the prestige, fame, good name and reputation of someone. This happens in three ways: calumny (false charges), detraction (undue revelation of another's defects) and rash judgment (thinking bad of others without real basis). The first and the third violate justice, but all three harm fraternal charity. In his exposition of vices opposed to the truth, St. Thomas Aquinas calls "pernicious (or mischievous) lies" those that injure others.[11]

It's so painful to be a victim of slander. People who make up stories or spill the beans about their neighbors' failings can't really imagine how it feels to be defamed until the tables are turned on them. We can easily pay our debts and have the car we bumped fixed. But it's difficult, let alone impossible, to restore the good name of someone unjustly accused. Once the bad seeds of smears are scattered to the four winds, it's very hard to rebuild good reputation. Whoever perpetrated the crime has the duty of restitution, to try to retract and eat one's words as much as he or she can. It's no joke that God has made this as the Eighth Commandment: *You shall not bear false witness against thy neighbor.*

Victor Hugo (1802-1885), a French poet and novelist, apparently had the custom of putting an extra vacant chair when he was with a friend or group of friends. It was his peculiar way of reminding them how someone absent would like to hear their conversation. Gossip can harm us as well as the person we talk about. When you hear someone pouring scorn on a fellow not present, you wonder what this talebearer might say about you behind your back. Rumormongering is seriously unjust for it casts a stigma on the good name of a person without him or her being there to defend oneself. That's why it's called backstabbing.

Before we open our mouths to share delicate information, we better think twice.[12] Talk less if only to avoid your tendency to exaggerate and reveal secrets!

What about the so-called "white lies" or those meant, for example, to avoid hurt feelings? A white lie may keep us in the good graces of a friend, but not for long. Over time it harms others. Think of a professor with a faint and hoarse voice who asks his students whether they can hear him well. "Those in the back row, do I speak loud enough?" They tell him, "It's perfectly clear, Sir," just to please him and he won't make an effort to do better. Say some nice words to your sister about her new hairdo even though you find it horrible, and she'll keep on sporting that hairstyle. So also if you opt not to call the attention of a friend stricken with halitosis, lest he might feel slighted, you're not acting as a true friend. He'll continue to go around with bad breath. It pays to be frank and honest even if it spells a little discomfort.

The etymology of the word "sincerity" is disputed, but all claims are interesting. One popular version traces its origin to two Latin terms—*sine* (without) and *cera* (wax). In the Roman Republic some unscrupulous craftsmen and marble workers apparently would cover the flaws in their sculptures using wax, much as modern woodworkers and antique dealers might rub wax to hide scratches in furniture. So *sine cera* became a guarantee for genuine, quality products. [13]

There's a modern version of such anomaly. When the price of petrol goes up, so too the costs of grocery items like cooking oil, toothpaste, noodles, sardines and milk. Transport fares of course hike up almost instantaneously. What about fast food chains? You may be surprised that a platter of pasta will still cost the same or even cheaper. Don't be fooled! It's the quantity that does the trick. The price may be the same, but now you only get a few spoonfuls of the dish. Or smaller pieces of chicken thigh, wing, or breast. At least you still get to see at once what you pay for. But "according to U.S. News & World Report, some manufacturers are selling us the same size packages we are accustomed to, but they are putting less of the product in the box. For example, a box of well-known detergent that once held 61 ounces now contains only 55. Same size box, less soap. How something is wrapped doesn't always show us what's on the inside. That's true with people as well. We can wrap ourselves up in the same packaging every day—nice clothes, big smile, friendly demeanor—yet still be less than what we appear to be."[14]

Tiny Children

More than once Jesus pointed to little kids as examples for us adults to imitate. (Cf. Mt 18:3) He didn't mean their immaturity, but their innocence. Children are simple creatures. Their candor is disarming and lays bare the entanglements of our life. Kids may be naughty at times, but their purity pricks our conscience for the many times we have been proud, sensual, dishonest and selfish. The soul of a little child is transparent, not tainted by malice and duplicity. Little boys and girls are incapable of keeping secrets, of telling a lie, of deceiving others. They don't weigh their words but say plainly what's on their mind. Their heart speaks through their laughter and tears, charms and tantrums. They're basically one piece. What you see is what you get.

A cousin of mine attended graduation rites at a theater hall. Tagging along was her little girl when the usher at the entrance stopped them, "Madam, sorry but kids below 7 years old aren't allowed inside." My cousin quickly assured him as she pushed her way through, "Oh, she's over 7." But before the attendant could do anything, the tiny tot butted in: "Mom, I just turned 6 yesterday! Remember my birthday cake?"

> In every little kid we see ourselves before we lost our innocence, before we messed up our life. His or her unadulterated mind and heart stir us to examine our past, and make us wish in retrospect that things were different, that we could begin all over again. We brush aside too often and too quickly what the small boys and girls tell us, when God sometimes talks to us through them. In these little creatures we should see the humility and simplicity of God.[15]

Being authentic and sincere adds human warmth to our relations and touches the hearts of people. They can sense if we are earnest or not. Pretenses are easy to detect. We build an atmosphere of confidence if we try to be ourselves, instead of projecting an image that's not real. We don't worry much how we appear or what others think about us, what we wear, how we speak and walk and move around. That's simplicity and naturalness. We act in the same way whether alone or in front of guests. I don't hide anything. There's nothing artificial in the way I act. I'm just the way I am, with my talents and shortcomings, fit of the sulks and cheerful moments.

If we want to say something, let's mean it and if we mean one thing, let's say it. Don't compliment a friend by saying you like his navy blue blazer if you really hate it! When you say "sorry" to someone, make sure you're truly sorry. If you can't commit to help, better not say anything that may raise false expectations. Failing to keep our promises is a form of lying.[16] No need to sugarcoat emails and personal notes with phrases lacking in candor; it's bad taste to say the least. A good rule of thumb would be to put ourselves in other people's shoes and think: "How would I feel if someone gives me a plastic smile or pretends to listen to me or pulls the wool over my eyes?" As the age-old dictum says, "Do not do unto others what you won't want others do unto you." Be simple, authentic and genuine! We should have a good reason to say and do whatever we say and do. Action based on firm belief is a trait of honest individuals.[17]

Simple individuals don't feel insecure or embarrassed by their dark skin, provincial accent, humble origins, modest means, physical defect, or low rank. They're not easily affected by "what they say about me." Sarcastic remarks aimed at us can hurt, but they hurt less when we're simple and humble. There's no reason to be ashamed of anything that's not an offense against God.[18]

Simplicity, though—being what you are—is not being barefaced and shameless, displaying one's turpitude. That's sincerity devoid of truth. Make no mistake about it. We can be "earnest" about our wrong ideas. A married man can claim to be genuinely "in love" with a woman not his wife. A patient in agony might be truly convinced that mercy killing is the best way to end one's suffering. A contractor can be serious about offering bribes to secure a project bid. Suicide bombers often blow themselves up thinking that it is a "holy" duty. And how many pregnant women "honestly believe" it's perfectly all right to abort their babies who may be born with congenital defects? Being honest with our feelings and beliefs doesn't necessarily mean we're doing the right thing.

> The world of publicity—advertising, propaganda, gossip—operates with the glow of sincerity and the almost complete absence of truth. Yet it is immensely successful because its façade of sincerity always manages to evoke in the masses at least some emotional response, however shallow that response may be. As face-to-face relationships diminish in an increasingly technologized society, it becomes easier for people to lie to each other. The "dangerous virtue" of sincerity, or vice, rather, induces moral paralysis. Such "sincerity" asks of a person only that he be himself, that is, remain completely unreformed and serenely indifferent to the circumstances that surround him.[19]

Sincerity is particularly important in the spiritual life. Our soul, perhaps darkened by pride, ignorance, worldliness and sensuality, will once again receive the light of God's grace and experience healing when we open up especially in the sacrament of Reconciliation.

We would also do well to lay bare our interior life in a heart to heart conversation with a spiritual director or anyone in a position to help us. We just have to be humble and shed our false defenses. *Veritas liberabit vos*—the truth will make you free. (Cf. Jn 8:32) Speak up! Release the burden weighing heavily on your heart! It has long kept your soul in the dark. Muster the courage to break the cycle of lies that only flatters Lucifer, the father of all lies! (Cf. Jn 8:44) Tear apart those fetters of self-imprisonment! Confide! Trust! Share your thoughts!

Is It The Truth?

Express your feelings! You have nothing to lose when you opt to be transparent! Sincerity heals deep and old wounds. It breeds serenity of mind. It cultivates human and spiritual maturity. Free of entanglements, an honest man is well able to focus on his work, concentrate in his prayer, do things purposefully and wear an authentic smile.

We become honest by dint of repeatedly telling the truth, until it becomes like our second nature. Time comes when almost effortlessly we speak plainly. Pure words flow out of our tongue as waters from a spring. People take us seriously. They hold us in high esteem. Our presence stirs up in others honest sentiments. Friends approach us to seek counsel. Integrity is indeed attractive.

So whenever you see the emblem of Rotary Club International, scour your memory to check on how you speak. *It is the truth?*

---

[1] *Birth of the Rotary 'Four-Way Test,'* in http://www.rotaract7030.org.

[2] *History of the 4-Way Test,* in http://thefourwaytest.com/history-of-the-four-way-test.

[3] *Ibid.*

[4] Leo J. Trese, *The Faith Explained.* Manila: Sinag-Tala Publishers, Inc., 2008, p. 286.

[5] Leo J. Trese, *Human But Holy: Getting To Know God, Yourself and Your Neighbor.* Manila: Sinag-Tala Publishers, Inc., 1999, p. 73.

[6] *Catechism of the Catholic Church,* no. 2486.

[7] *Code of Canon Law,* no. 1101.

[8] James Socias and Aurelio Fernandez, *Our Moral Life in Christ: A Basic Course on Moral Theology*. Chicago: Midwest Theological Forum, Inc., 1997, p. 339.

[9] *Ibid.*, p. 337.

[10] St. Josemaría Escrivá, *Furrow*, no. 602.

[11] St. Thomas Aquinas, *Summa Theologiae*, IIa-IIae, q. 110, a. 1.

[12] http://www.artofmanliness.com/2008/04/13/the-virtuous-life-sincerity.

[13] http://ancienthistory.about.com/od/etymology/f/Sincere.htm.

[14] http://virtuefirst.org/virtues/sincerity.

[15] Henry Bocala, *Arise and Walk: How Does Your Christian Faith Fit in a Confused World?* Manila: Daughters of St. Paul, 2007, p. 79.

[16] Charles, Belmonte, (ed.), *Faith Seeking Understanding: A Complete Course on Theology*, vol. II. Manila: Studium Theologiae Foundation, Inc., 1997, p. 161.

[17] http://virtuefirst.org/virtues/sincerity.

[18] Juan Luis Lorda, *The Virtues of Holiness: The Basics of Spiritual Struggle*. New York: Scepter Publishers, 2010, p. 42.

[19] Donald De Marco, *The Heart of Virtue*. San Francisco, Ignatius Press, 1996, pp. 209-210.

Chapter Eight

NO LOITERING ALLOWED

The verb "loiter" is defined by the Oxford dictionary as "to stand or wait around without apparent purpose." The word is synonymous with "idle," "loaf," "kill time," "mooch about," "tarry," or "dawdle." All these connote one idea—to hang around in a bored or listless manner or while the hours away doing nothing.

If we see the notice "No Loitering Allowed" posted visibly in a subway station, mall entrance, church gate, university corridor or hospital lobby, know that the world is teeming with lazybones, good-for-nothing fellows who don't seem to know what to do in life. They bum around, wandering aimlessly from place to place and crowd out those who have a real purpose for being there. The placard sends them a clear message: Stay away! This isn't a place for unproductive people. I think the signage "No Loitering Allowed" should carry a tag line: "You Better Do Something Useful!" or "Make Good Use of Your Time!"

We're not talking here about the unemployed, vagrants, homeless and scavengers who are victims of social injustice; they loiter perhaps to find ways for survival. Rather, we refer to those folks who loiter for sheer love of comfort. You may not see them lingering out there on the side streets. But their day is replete with useless delays, idle stops and dull pauses. There's reluctance to work, a tendency to shun duties and a proclivity for an easygoing lifestyle.

That's the case of a student who cuts classes to play computer games; an employee who chitchats intermittently during office hours; a security guard who dozes off while on duty; or a messenger wont to make detours while on official errands. We, too, "loiter" when we spend *too much* time reading the newspapers, watching TV, taking a coffee break, surfing the Internet, or window-shopping, aware that we have other pressing matters to do.

Ut Operaretur

Everybody works. Or almost everybody! It's the most normal thing for us to be occupied with certain tasks. Not only the able-bodied work but even the "disabled," such as a foot painter or a blind masseur. Work takes up most of our waking hours. It's a daily grind. From the moment we jump out of bed till we call it a day, our hands are full. It's the natural vocation of the human person to labor, to "be fruitful" and "dominate the earth" (Gen 1:28). In a sense, you and I were born in order to work—*ut operaretur* (Gen 2:15), just as the birds are born in order to fly (Cf. Job 5:7). Saint Josemaría, modern day saint and champion of the hidden value of ordinary life said that "work is a magnificent reality; an inexorable law which, one way or another, binds everyone."[1]

Archeologists and anthropologists aren't so exact when we humans learned to create fire, make rope and tie knots. But there's consensus about the origin of work because it has always been there; it coexists with life. As Richard Donkin says in his book, *The History of Work*, the development of tools predates any understanding of work as a concept. Things simply had to be done. Work was a way of life.[2] It still is to this day.

If we ask high school students what they want to be when they grow up, one might say, "I like to become a doctor." Another would probably choose to be an engineer or a teacher or a politician or a banker or a pilot. In other words, we define our future normally in terms of a professional path, in categories of work. Ironically, a high school in southwestern Sweden planned to pay its students who register perfect attendance because of increasing truancy across the country, the school principal said.[3] I didn't know that attending classes could earn stipends. Do we need incentives to do what we're supposed to do in the first place? We better have clear ideas. First and foremost, owe it to our own self to do our best.

A hefty salary may prompt us to perform well. We may feel great doing our job. But there's a deeper reason why we need to set our hands to the plough. Work is a requirement of human dignity. It adds to our personal worth. Hence, industriousness is a virtue we ought to practice. And we hang on even if we find the present job difficult (*bonum arduum*, arduous good, according to St. Thomas Aquinas). Whatever helps us shape up, whatever spells personal betterment, is worth the effort. In classical ethics the virtue of diligence is illustrated with a woman holding a whip and spurs, signifying the drive to steadfastly move forward through one's means.

But work transcends the sphere of the individuals. Work is bound up with our duty to contribute to the common good, to build up society.[4] This is the core of social responsibility. We labor to help make this world a better place to live in. All past inventions and discoveries are the common patrimony of mankind. We enjoy the fruits of what our forefathers have toiled for. No need to reinvent the wheel, we know. But I wonder, "What can we contribute for posterity?"

Despite the fatigue it brings, work ennobles us. In a sense, it frees our spirit from the domination of matter. Each task accomplished, every product of our hands, is linked up with the joy of victory over material things and over oneself. The working person straddles, as it were, heaven and earth. When done with a pure motive, every task at hand has a redeeming value. Human labor is a path to heaven, a means of union with God. Somehow the world is an unfinished project and its Creator calls us to cooperate in His creative and salvific mission. No matter how humble, our work has an infinite value in His eyes.[5]

Do It Now!

Time is ticking by and we have a full agenda for the day. Some of these are probably carry overs from days past. Let's work double time and catch up on unfinished business! Things that drag on are like deadweights that can stall other projects in the pipeline. It is not good to postpone matters we can already get over with.[6] Unnecessary delays are bad work habits. My niece posted on her Facebook wall a photo of her wrist watch, its hour and minute hands pointing to a red and silver engraving that said: *Do It Now!*

We should also avoid voluntary distractions that disrupt our tempo. Stay focused, work intensely for hours on end! Competitive multinationals take note even of the minutes spent by their staff in the toilet, cafeteria or on the phone.

It pays to be time-conscious but without rushing through in a panic. We're able to multiply our time when we follow a schedule and work efficiently. Set your priorities! First things first! Urgent matters may have to wait though, if only because they need a more thorough consideration. Empty that paper tray of pending items! Check your Inbox! If you're worn-out after a hard day's work, it's a good sign. That means your energies have been well spent. We're filled with serenity when goals are met. It's restful. "Those who have missed the joy of work, of a job well done, have missed something very important."[7] So says William Bennett in *The Book of Virtues*, a no. 1 New York Times bestseller.

When we love what we do, we breeze through it. Difficulties are easily overcome. We don't mind the sweat; we're only too willing to do the donkeywork and work our fingers to the bone. No need for a shot in the arm, but that's welcome as an added bonus. We're self-propelled and we take initiatives. The call of duty urges us on. We give our best and even go the extra mile. Mind and body may be tired, but we can hack it. Every hour, every minute counts. There's a sense of fulfillment and we prod others to keep at it. That's when we enjoy doing our tasks.

But this isn't always the case. The daily toil can sap our energy. We get exhausted; we grow weary. Exertion drains us physically and mentally. For some people, tiredness is compounded by emotional hang-ups. A sense of monotony can also slow us down. Plus we all have a fair share of lapses, flops and letdowns. And we can have a really bad day. Blame it on a tactless colleague, a rigid boss, an inept team, last-minute changes or a series of deadlines! At times we wonder if we're making any difference and if it's worth all the pain. "Am I in the right place?" Or "Is this fair?" Or "Am I happy doing all these?" In any case, try to help create a healthy working environment and stick to your duties!

A business firm shared helpful tips to budding entrepreneurs using reverse psychology. It circulated a poster revealing the "secrets" to a successful business venture: 1) Sit down and wait for opportunities to come; 2) Talk about your bad luck to others; 3) Be content with your achievements; 4) Lament the difficult times; 5) Depend on recommendations; and 6) Hope for favorable circumstances. It's rather obvious that these are the recipes for a complete business failure.

Let's put duties over preferences. We might be busy with the wrong things. Too many people are occupied with matters that were not meant to be their concern and so deadlines pile up. They like to cram, saying that pressures bring out their best. But it's a convenient excuse for sloth and disorder. Scatterbrains lack focus and intensity. They call it quits no sooner than they begin something. They hop from one thing to another, leaving a trail of sloppy, haphazard jobs. Kids are like that somehow. Their span of attention lasts no longer than ten minutes. Beyond that, one had better use magic tricks or wear a clown costume to make them to stay put.

Our initial enthusiasm can peter out when we do the same thing over and over. We're not surprised if at times we lack the motivation to finish what we've begun. But the situation isn't really as bad as we imagine. Many others have gone through it before, so why can't we? Everyone has a share of responsibilities. Toughies take challenges as opportunities for growth. It's a question of perseverance, of fortitude, of having the right attitude. Just work on! Keep quiet and concentrate! Libraries put up "Maintain Silence" notices to make sure people are able to work and study well in a conducive environment. Conquer boredom! Do a little sacrifice! Honor your commitments! Your credibility is at stake. People expect you to deliver results. They count on you; they appreciate your valuable inputs. Yes, you're making a positive contribution. So show them the loyalty that only you can give!

There is no shortcut to success. It comes by dint of hard work. Sports legends, for example, are not born champions. They sweat it out; they train with rigor and discipline. John R. Wooden (a.k.a. the "Wizard of Westwood") was an American basketball player and coach. He won ten NCAA national championships in a 12-year period—seven in a row—as head coach of UCLA, a record feat. He is famous for his superb ability to motivate players and his pyramid of success, of which the foundation is industriousness. Explaining his pyramid, coach Wooden said, "You've got to work really hard. There's no substitute for work. None. Worthwhile things come only from real work."[8]

Work-Life Balance

If there are people who loiter (i.e., rest too much) and work too little, there are also those who work a bit too much and rest too little. Workaholics, that's what they're called. Just as alcoholics are addicted to alcohol, workaholics are addicted to work. It may be their way of escaping reality, of running away from household troubles. They'd rather work overtime than be home early. So, too, there are prisoners of success—men and women who love their job so much and the rewards that come along. They are "married" to their careers. In both cases, other important aspects of life suffer. There is less time for the family, social isolation, neglect of health, and prayer and worship are sidelined. Industriousness is a positive trait, but to work compulsively hard and long is a serious disorder.[9] Anything excessive is bad.

But the problem isn't just a matter of personal attitudes. In many ways, today's corporate culture is not family-friendly and this is reflected in company policies, management styles, organizational structures and work shifts. Business firms hire the best minds, give them optimum training, and shower them with untold benefits only to kill them with work. A career woman wrote these lines to a management consulting company: "I am a burnt-out, overworked professional as well as a guilt-ridden mother...My goal: to earn a 'decent' and stable living with the ability to spend quality time with my children..." I work "as a high-level project manager for a company with a very aggressive corporate culture. Over the last couple of years I have become fed up with the constant push to perform at higher and higher levels...I have come to realize that I would prefer to 'scale down.'"[10]

The experience of this woman is shared by millions of other people whose lives are swallowed up by a demanding career. Our generation is fast-paced, moves by nanoseconds, driven by professional ambition in a never-ending rat race to the top. An overly competitive environment that requires an increasingly higher productivity and better performance from employees tends to erode our sense of humanity. Some even forget to take a shower or brush their teeth in the morning rush. At what cost? Rising incidence of depression, anxiety and stress-related disorders. The alarming trend gave rise to calls for a healthy work-life balance. Society is in want of a correct work perspective, a proper equilibrium between work itself and the larger scope of life.[11]

Are you capable of multi-tasking like receiving phone calls while typing? You may do so if you really are able to handle two or more jobs at a time. But chances are, one's attention gets too dispersed, work quality suffers, human contexts are switched and time is wasted. For many experts, multi-tasking is a myth. Just do one thing at time!

There is a valuable lesson in this children's rhyme:

> *Work while you work,*
> *Play while you play;*
> *One thing each time,*
> *That is the way.*
>
> *All that you do,*
> *Do with your might;*
> *Things done by halves*
> *Are not done right.*[12]

Hands, Heart and Head

To be diligent doesn't always imply doing heavy work. At home it can mean washing the dishes, closing the gates, emptying the wastebasket, mowing the lawn, feeding the pet dog and the like. There are so many things that aren't urgent, but have to be done just the same. We thus need to put time into all these, making ourselves available. Don't leave everything for the handyman or domestic help to do! If you can lock the doors or replace the toilet paper yourself, why wait for the others?

To be productive, though, we must try to forget our petty concerns and rid our minds of egotistic thoughts that set us adrift and deceive us about being the center of the universe. Disordered self-love isolates us from other people, including our loved ones. We no longer reach out to them, nor can they reach us out, enclosed as we are in our self-made enclave. It's time to break out of that eggshell called the self. Work is intrinsically service-oriented. It manifests our social nature, our vocation to charity. Through work we can make a difference in other people's lives.[13] We just have to employ our hands, heart and head.

The 20th century saw technological advances grow by leaps and bounds. Electrification brought light and power to our homes, making household chores a lot easier and more efficient. Engineering innovations like resistance heating and small motors gave rise to electric stoves, fans and irons, vacuum cleaners, washing machines, and dryers. Then there were pop-up toasters and Freon-operated refrigerators. General Electric introduced the first self-cleaning electric oven in 1963. Singer launched Athena 2000 in 1978, an electronic sewing machine capable of multiple stitches. These machines can be set, pre-programmed to work on their own and turn off without human presence.[14] All these—to say nothing of the subsequent computer, digital and nanotech revolutions—meant laborsaving and countless man-hours freed for other tasks.

Productivity still belongs to humans. These smart machines would be of little use if we choose to stay idle. Instruments of work are just that, tools to be used by rational beings. They're just as good (or as lousy) as the hands that employ them. Let me paraphrase the words of Microsoft co-founder Bill Gates. The first rule, he said, of any technology use is that automation applied to an efficient operation will magnify the efficiency. The second is that automation applied to an inefficient operation will magnify the inefficiency.[15] Don't believe that robots will render brain and brawn work superfluous; it's a silly proposition of those who just like to loiter around.

What enriches us as persons are not the cutting-edge gadgets that supposedly facilitate things for us, but the labor of our bare hands. An artist can really take pride with his own masterpiece, but not quite with an artwork churned out by Photoshop. And if we find product ads proudly showcasing a *handcrafted* rocking chair, *homemade* ice cream, *organic* vegetables or car *hand-wash*, it's because people value more anything molded with human touch and care, than items mass-produced in factories. "There are no menial jobs, only menial attitudes."[16]

God gave each of us talents and natural abilities. We better put them to good use. Let's not squander the gifts we've received. The least we can do to show our gratitude is make them bear fruits. That means work.

At the end of our earthly journey, everyone will be asked to render an account of what we've done with those investments from on high. Remember that man in the Gospel who hid the money entrusted to him? He got a dressing-down from his master. "'You wicked and slothful servant! You knew that I reap where I have not sowed, and gather where I have not winnowed. Then you ought to have invested my money with the bankers, and at my coming I should have received what was my own with interest.'" (Mt 25:26-27)

In Dante's *Divine Comedy*, Hell or Inferno (Cantos 1-14) is divided into major groupings and circles. Interestingly, the souls consigned to the fifth circle include the lazy or the sullen, whose punishment is being trapped in the hazy Stygian marsh (from River Styx in Greek mythology) where they do what they did in the present life—nothing.[17]

Indolent. Slothful. Apathetic. Laggard. Lazy people ruin their lives by sheer inaction. They're reluctant to take the trouble to do things. They refuse to employ their hands, even just to bring the food to their mouths. Many of them fall prey to poverty and become social parasites. Scarcity prods them to knock on their neighbor's door begging for help. But only those who help themselves deserve compassion. Saint Paul forewarned the Christians of work-shy people who exploit fraternal spirit for their daily sustenance. The Apostle of the Gentiles minced no words, if only to teach them a lesson: "If any one will not work, let him not eat." (2 Thess 3:10)

What's the best antidote to laziness? Steadfast application. Industry. Assiduous work. Personal discipline. Good work ethics. The will to serve. Drive for excellence. Take the advice of New York Times bestselling author Allison Brennan: "Dig until you hit rock. Then take out that jackhammer and go a little deeper." If you look behind, there's a placard that says, "No Loitering Allowed."

---

[1] St. Josemaría Escrivá, *Friends of God*, no. 57.

[2] Richard Donkin, *The History of Work*. New York: Palgrave Macmillan, May 2010, p. 8.

[3] *The Australian*, 16 January 2003, p. 16.

[4] Joseph De Torre, *Work, Culture, Liberation: The Social Teaching of the Church*. Quezon City (Philippines): Vera Reyes, Inc., 1985, p. 48.

[5] Stefan Cardinal Wyszynski, *Work*. Chicago: Scepter Publishers, Ltd., 1960, pp. 96-103.

[6] Juan Luis Lorda, *The Virtues of Holiness: The Basics of Spiritual Struggle*. New York: Scepter Publishers, 2010, p. 69.

[7] William J. Bennett (ed.), *The Book of Virtues: A Treasury of Great Moral Stories*. New York: Simon & Schuster, 1993, p. 347.

[8] http://earnpurpleinc.blogspot.com/2013/06/industriousness-john-r-wooden-pyramid.html.

[9] Fernando Bartolomé, *The Work Alibi: When It's Harder to Go Home*. Boston: Harvard Business Review on Work and Life Balance, President and Fellows of Harvard College, 2000, pp. 83-84.

[10] http://www.joanlloyd.com/Your-Career/Burned-out-mom-seeks-less-demanding-job.aspx.

[11] Henry Bocala, *Mending A Broken Society: What Happens When We Forget Who We Are?* Manila: Daughters of St. Paul, 2012, p. 75.

[12] Bennett, *op. cit.*, p. 355.

[13] Linda Kavelin Popov, *The Family Virtues Guide*. New York: Penguin Group, 1997, p. 237.

[14] http://www.greatachievements.org/?id=3768. Copyright 2014 by National Academy of Engineering.

[15] www.brainyquote.com/quotes/authors/b/bill_gates.html.

[16] Bennett, *op. cit.*, p. 348.

[17] *Notes to Dante's The Divine Comedy: Inferno*, in http://www.poetryintranslation.com/PITBR/Italian/DantnotesInf.htm and http://www.studyflashcard.com/flashcards/classic-literature-dante-s-inferno-cantos-1-14/deck/15.

 **About Leonine Publishers**

Leonine Publishers LLC makes fine Catholic literature available to Catholics throughout the English-speaking world. Leonine Publishers offers an innovative "hybrid" approach to book publication that helps authors as well as readers. Please visit our web site at www.leoninepublishers.com to learn more about us. Browse our online bookstore to find more solid Catholic titles to uplift, challenge, and inspire.

Our patron and namesake is Pope Leo XIII, a prudent, yet uncompromising pope during the stormy years at the close of the 19th century. Please join us as we ask his intercession for our family of readers and authors.

Do you have a book inside you? Visit our web site today. Leonine Publishers accepts manuscripts from Catholic authors like you. If your book is selected for publication, you will have an active part in the production process. This book is an example of our growing selection of literature for the busy Catholic reader of the 21st century.

www.leoninepublishers.com

www.ingramcontent.com/pod-product-compliance
Lightning Source LLC
Chambersburg PA
CBHW031359040426
42444CB00005B/353